"Now Jesus did many other signs in the presence of his disciples, which are not written in this book; but these are written that you may believe that Jesus is the Christ, the Son of God, and that believing you may have life in his name."

(The Gospel According to John 20:30-31)

That You May Believe

MIRACLES AND FAITH
THEN AND NOW

COLIN BROWN

Wipf & Stock
PUBLISHERS
Eugene, Oregon

Wipf and Stock Publishers
199 West 8th Avenue, Suite 3
Eugene, Oregon 97401

That You May Believe
Miracles and Faith Then and Now
By Brown, Colin
Copyright©1985 by Brown, Colin
ISBN: 0-9653517-4-2
Publication date 8/8/1996
Previously published by Wm. B. Eerdmans Publishing Co., 1985

Contents

III. CAN WE EXPECT MIRACLES TODAY?

Introduction

"What do you think, Reverend? Should we go?"

A CRISIS OF FAITH

Here was a question the seminary had not prepared me for. I had just graduated with my degree in theology. I was the proud possessor of two degrees and was eager to embark on yet another. If she had asked me about the date of the exodus, the finer points of the Arian controversy, or some other scholarly matter, I could have talked for an hour. But this was a question for which I was unprepared.

"Should we go?" She was talking about her teenage daughter. The girl was pretty, able, and intelligent—but she walked with a limp. The mother was asking me about the healing service. We did not have anything of the sort in our church, but they did in the church down the road. They had them once a month, and in the weeks to come I was asked the same question over and over again by different people.

It was 1958. I was newly ordained, and I was on the staff of a large parish near Nottingham in the English Midlands. Ministers are supposed to know everything, or so I thought. It wasn't just a matter of personal pride. It was bound up with the belief that Christianity had an answer to all of life's questions and that ministers were there to help people. If I failed on this one, I was letting down Christ.

But I couldn't give a straight answer. For one thing I hadn't thought very deeply about miracles or healing. They simply hadn't come up in my academic courses. So there I was without much help to offer.

In the weeks and months that followed I began to ask questions of my own. I also met the minister who held the healing services. He even spoke at our monthly ministers' meeting. "You are preaching only half a gospel," he said. "You preach that Christ died for people's sins. But that is only half the story. Jesus not only preached, he also healed people. If Jesus healed then, why aren't you carrying out his healing ministry today?"

The minister reminded us of the words of Matthew. Jesus "cast out the spirits with a word, and healed all who were sick. This was to fulfil what was spoken by the prophet Isaiah, 'He took our infirmities and bore our diseases' " (Matthew 8:16-17). Did not Jesus command his disciples to heal the sick? Is not Jesus Christ "the same yesterday and today and forever" (Hebrews 13:8)? Why then were we disobedient? Why then were we failing the sick and needy all around us? Why were we failing Christ?

The questions hit me hard. I searched my soul and prayed. I also began to read. One of the books I got hold of was B. B. Warfield's *Miracles: Yesterday and Today, True and False* (reprint Grand Rapids: Eerdmans, 1954). Warfield was one of my theological heroes. He was a redoubtable champion of biblical inerrancy and a staunch defender of Reformed theology. From 1887 to 1921, when he died, Warfield was Professor of Didactic and Polemical Theology at Princeton Theological Seminary.

Warfield's book first appeared in 1918. It was an incomparable inventory of objections to the miraculous in the history of the church through the ages. Warfield believed in miracles, but only those recorded in the Bible. In his view, miracles ceased with the apostles. Their purpose was to accredit Christ and the apostles in founding the church. Once this purpose was fulfilled, miracles were no longer needed. As Warfield guided his readers through exotic stories from the early church and the Middle Ages to the happenings at Lourdes, the vagaries of the Irvingites, and Mary Baker Eddy's explanation of why she found it necessary to visit a dentist, he left them in no doubt about the power of wishful thinking in matters of religion.

Another book that came into my hands was D. J. West's *Eleven Lourdes Miracles* (London: Duckworth, 1957). West was a doctor, an expert researcher, and an independent investigator. Of the thousands of ailing pilgrims who have made their way to Lourdes for healing, relatively few have returned cured, and only a handful of these have been recognized by the Catholic Church as cases of authentic miracles. West's book was an examination of eleven cases of healing between 1943 and 1952. All were recognized as authentic miracles, attributed to the intervention of the Blessed Virgin Mary. The Lourdes Medical Bureau published medical dossiers on them. But West concluded, "In no case was the evidence really satisfactory, and in certain cases the evidence suggested a perfectly natural alternative explanation" (p. 97).

Part of the trouble was the incompleteness of the case histories, which often contained interpretations instead of facts documented by X-rays and lab tests. But these were among the best-attested cases of healing. If West was skeptical about these, what would he make of my minister friend down the road who claimed regular results from his healing services? And what was one to make of the role of the Virgin Mary in all this?

If Warfield and West were skeptical about modern miracles, Henry Frost's *Miraculous Healing* (reprint London: Marshall, Morgan and Scott, 1951) struck a different note. It would not have pleased the thorough skeptic, but neither did it give unqualified support to the advocates of faith healing. My copy of Frost's book contains an appreciation by D. Martyn Lloyd-Jones. No author could hope for a higher commendation. Martyn Lloyd-Jones was the greatest preacher of his day and had given up a brilliant career in medicine to become a minister. Lloyd-Jones said of Frost's book: "It is easily and incomparably the best book I have ever read on this subject.

... Many times I have been asked to write myself on this theme. I have always replied by saying that Henry W. Frost has already dealt with the matter in what I regard as a final and conclusive manner" (p. 7).

In the meantime I began to make inquiries of my own. When I asked about healing services I kept getting the same answers. The conversations went something like this:

Question: "Did you see people healed at the services?"

Answer: "Well, people were helped a lot, and some of them got better."

Question: "I mean, did you ever see something that you would call a miracle? Something that could not be put down to medical help, remission, or recovery taking its own course? Something that could not be put down to psychology? Something that was clearly a case of supernatural healing?"

It was at this point that my questions always seemed to get stuck. The only straightforward answers were negative.

As I look back, the events of the 1950s seem to be a lifetime away. I never did learn what became of the lady who asked about the healing service and her daughter. But I do know what happened to my cousin David. He died. In a sense he never really grew up. When we were small we used to play together. I liked him, but most of the time I could not make out what he was saying. He didn't talk like the other boys and girls. He didn't go to school with them either. He just stayed at home and played and had occasional visits from a special teacher. When he died people said that it was a blessing. By then he was in his twenties. My aunt and uncle had tried Christian Science for a while. They had taken David to a nationally known faith healer. But things continued much the same.

I never once heard my aunt and uncle complain. They were ordinary folk—in one sense. They were extraordinary in another sense. To many people the care of a mentally defective child would have been a devastating blow. Yet it was David's death that seemed more crushing. There was no miracle of healing for David but death itself. Yet he was happy in the twilight zone in which he lived. No doubt many agonizing prayers of faith had been offered for David, but no miraculous transformation occurred. Week by week the family went to the Methodist Chapel in the village and found grace and strength to get them through another week.

THREE QUESTIONS

Sooner or later every minister and every Christian has to face the question of healing. But it is only one of a larger set of questions. For some people the big question is whether Christianity has reserves of power for all to tap if only they have faith and go about it in the right way. But for other people the very idea of the miraculous is the real problem.

Civilization in both the East and the West is dominated by science and technology. The advance of knowledge has shown the inadequacy of so many ideas handed down from the past. No thinking person can escape the challenge of modern knowledge to his or her views of God and the world. Can we really believe in miracles today? What are we to make of the Bible stories about Jesus? Did he really do the things he is supposed to have done? Who was Jesus anyway?

In this book I have tried to grapple with these issues. I have set myself three main questions, and I have divided the book into three corresponding parts.

I. *Can We Still Believe in Miracles?*
II. *What Do the Miracle Stories Tell Us about Jesus?*
III. *Can We Expect Miracles Today?*

Part I asks: *Can We Still Believe in Miracles?* The six chapters in this part of the book deal with the philosophical debate about miracles. Chapter 1 looks at changing attitudes toward miracles. At one time miracles were part of the foundation of Christian apologetics, but now many people feel that the miracle stories are something for which the church has to apologize. Chapter 2 examines the classic objections to miracles, as stated by the eighteenth-century skeptic David Hume. Chapter 3 looks more closely at the dynamics of the argument. It introduces the important ideas of "analogy" and "frames of reference" that play key roles in deciding whether a story or a report is credible. Chapter 4 looks at C. S. Lewis's classic argument for belief in miracles. Chapter 5 asks: "What Sort of World Do We Live In?" It tries to envisage how miracles are conceivable in relation to a scientific view of the world and in relation to the God of the Bible. Chapter 6 concludes the first part of the book with an attempt to define miracles from the philosophical as well as from the biblical standpoint.

Part II asks: *What Do the Miracle Stories Tell Us about Jesus?* This part of the book begins with Chapter 7, which contains a sketch of how scholars in the last two hundred years have tried to reconstruct a picture of Jesus by explaining away or leaving out the miraculous. I have called this chapter "The Quest of the Unhistorical Jesus." Chapter 8 is entitled "Unscrambling the Puzzle." It examines some of the misconceptions of both opponents and defenders of the miracle stories. Chapters 9–11 are devoted to "Remaking the Puzzle." I attempt to do this in three steps. Step 1 (Chapter 9) deals with Mark's picture of Jesus, step 2 (Chapter 10) examines the pictures of Matthew, Luke, and John, and step 3 considers the emerging picture of Jesus in the light of our examination of the miracle stories.

Part III returns to the question with which I began: *Can We Expect Miracles Today?* If Jesus healed people as he went about Galilee, Judea, and Jerusalem, should we not expect similar miracles today? Is the church failing in its duty if it does not carry out a vigorous healing ministry? Are there vast reserves of divine power ready to heal the chronically sick if only we have faith and understand the right spiritual techniques? Chapter 12 asks the question "Health and Wealth for All?" It takes note of studies of evidence for healing. It also examines arguments in favor of miraculous healing today and reviews their biblical basis. Chapter 13 draws the argument together. It poses the question "What can we expect of God?" and gives the answer "My Grace Is Sufficient."

I have written this book for my lay friends. I have tried to face the issues fairly and squarely. At the same time I have tried to avoid burdening readers with technical detail and the academic apparatus of documentation and footnotes that scholars rightly require in learned treatises. Readers who wish to follow through the arguments of Parts I and II of this book will find them elaborated and documented in my larger book *Miracles and the Critical Mind* (Grand Rapids: Eerdmans, 1984). Those who wish to delve more deeply into the question of healing will find suggestions for further reading in A Note on Books at the end of this book.

In writing this book I owe debts of gratitude to many people. Above all I am indebted to the love and patience of my wife Olive, who has read and reread the typescript and made countless improvements. Two of my colleagues at Fuller Theological Seminary read the entire first draft and helped me enormously in my revision. They are Dr. Robert P. Meye, Dean of the School of Theology and Professor of New Testament Interpretation, and Dr. Paul G. Hiebert, Professor of Anthropology and South Asian Studies. Other friends have helped me with various parts of the book. My sister-in-law and her husband, Joan and B. MacDonald Hennell, read the first part. Dr. George Gay, Senior Associate Professor of New Testament and Acting Director of Hispanic Ministries, and Frances Hiebert helped me with the last part. I am also much indebted to Jon Pott, Vice-President and Editor-in-Chief of Wm. B. Eerdmans Publishing Company, and his staff for their advice and help. I am especially grateful to Janet Gathright and Mariam Thalos of the Fuller School of Theology Word

Processing Office for word-processing my typescript. Needless to say, none of these friends should be held responsible for the flaws in this book or the ideas it contains.

I dedicate this book in love and gratitude to my parish church in which my wife serves as a Lay Reader and in which I serve as Associate—St. Mark's Episcopal Church, Altadena, California.

COLIN BROWN

I / Can We Still Believe in Miracles?

1 / From Foundation to Crutch to Cross

Miracle was once the foundation of all apologetics, then it became an apologetic crutch, and today it is not infrequently regarded as a cross for apologetics to bear. (Reinhold Seeberg, *Realenzyklopädie für protestantische Theologie und Kirche*, XXI, 562)

In days gone by, miracles were seen as clear-cut proof of divine intervention. Christians answered their critics and persecutors by pointing to the miracles performed by Jesus and his followers. Miracles were like God's seal of approval. They were a kind of guarantee, for all to see, of God's backing. But today many people are unsure which side the miracle stories are really on. They see them as more of a liability than an asset. At best they have changed from being a foundation for faith to being an object of faith. At worst they have to be apologized for. Miracles seem to belong to the realm of myth and fantasy. They do not seem to have a place in the technological world of computers, body transplants, and space shuttles. From being a foundation for the faith, they seem to have become a cross that the defender of the faith has to bear.

THE CLASSIC ARGUMENT

New Testament Preaching. From the earliest days of the Christian church miracles have played a key part in preaching and apologetics. The Acts of the Apostles paints a picture of life in the newly founded church. On the day of Pentecost when the church was launched the apostle Peter bluntly addressed his fellow Jews:

> "Men of Israel, hear these words: Jesus of Nazareth, a man attested to you by God with mighty works and wonders and signs which God did through him in your midst as you yourselves know—this Jesus, delivered up according to the definite plan and foreknowledge of God, you crucified and killed by the hands of lawless men. But God raised him up, having loosed the pangs of death, because it was not possible for him to be held by it." (Acts 2:22-24)

Some time later Peter repeated the same argument to Cornelius and his companions. He spoke of

> "How God anointed Jesus of Nazareth with the Holy Spirit and with power; how he went about doing good and healing all that were oppressed by the devil, for God was with him. And we are witnesses to all that he did both in the country of the Jews and in Jerusalem. They put him to death by hanging him on a tree; but God raised him on the third day and made him manifest; not to all the people but to us who were chosen by God as witnesses, who ate and drank with him after he rose from the dead." (Acts 10:38-41)

A number of things are striking about these two reports of Peter's preaching. First of all, there is the timing. The words were spoken on two of the most momentous occasions in the history of the church. The first occasion was Pentecost, when the Spirit was poured out and the church was opened up to all Jews who responded to Peter's call to repent and be baptized in the name of Jesus Christ. They were promised the forgiveness of sins and the gift of the Spirit. The second occasion was when the church was opened up to non-Jews. The Spirit fell on all who heard Peter. It was now clear that anyone who responded to God's Word and had received the Spirit— whether Jewish or not—was fit to be received into the church.

In neither case was anyone converted simply by argument. But in neither case was anyone converted without argument. A feature of the argument in both cases was the characterization of Jesus as one through whom God wrought mighty works. These works were well attested. Moreover, there is a close connection between Jesus' works, his death, and his resurrection. We shall get back to this point later.

Catholic and Protestant Apologetics. The theme of Jesus' miracles reechoed in Christian preaching and teaching through the centuries. Origen, the greatest apologist and theologian of the third century, observed that "without miracles and wonders" the apostles "would not have persuaded those who heard new doctrines and new teachings to leave their traditional religion and accept the apostles' teaching at the risk of their lives." Justin, who was martyred in Rome in the middle of the second century, spoke of how Jesus' actions "challenged the men of his time to recognize him." In the fourth century Gregory of Nyssa stated bluntly, "His very miracles have convinced us of his deity."

Similar conclusions could easily be multiplied from Athanasius and Augustine in the early church to Thomas Aquinas and his contemporaries in the Middle Ages. They can be found in the Reformers and their successors down to Christian writers in our own day. Although they have disagreed on many issues, orthodox Catholicism and mainstream Protestantism have seen pretty well eye to eye on the subject of miracles.

The First Vatican Council of the Roman Catholic Church (1869-70) declared that since miracles and prophecies "so excellently display God's omnipotence and limitless knowledge, they constitute the surest signs of divine revelation, signs that are suitable to everyone's understanding." If we want a spokesman for Protestant theology, we cannot do better than the great Reformer of Geneva in the sixteenth century, John Calvin. Calvin reflected on the theme of miracles at several places in his *Institutes of the Christian Religion.* (For details see Calvin's "Prefatory Address to King

Francis"; I, viii, 5-7; I, xiii, 13; IV, xiv, 18; and IV, xix, 6 and 18.)

For Calvin, the teaching of Moses in the Old Testament was "sanctioned for all time" by the miracles that he wrought. He smote the rock, and it produced water. The giving of the manna and the signs and wonders linked with the exodus from Egypt were acts of God that all could recognize. In the same way, the miracles performed by the apostles in the early church served to *attest* their witness and *seal* the gospel that they preached (see Acts 14:3; Romans 15:19; Hebrews 2:4).

Calvin was aware that the argument might appear to prove too much. For if Moses could do miracles and the apostles perform signs and wonders, what difference was there between them and Jesus? Calvin met the difficulty by admitting that the miracles of the prophets and apostles were equal to and similar to those of Jesus. But whereas the miracles of the prophets and apostles were temporary gifts of God, the miracles of Jesus showed forth his divinity. In him all the fullness of divinity dwelt bodily (Colossians 2:9). "How plainly and clearly," declared Calvin, "is his deity shown in miracles!"

THE CLASSICAL OBJECTIONS

Can We Be Sure of the Evidence? The apparent similarity between Jesus' miracles and those performed by other characters in the Bible was not the only difficulty Calvin faced. Could it be that some of the miracles recorded in the Bible were not real miracles at all? Maybe the acts of Moses were not genuine miracles. Calvin quelled such doubts by pointing out that all the miracles that Moses did were done in full view of the public. If there had been a trick of some kind, surely someone would have spotted it. Some of the people might be fooled some of the time, but surely not all the people all the time.

If this answer satisfied Calvin and pious believers of subsequent generations, it did not satisfy those of a more critical frame of mind. After all, the books of the Old Testament simply give the views of their authors. Who was to check on them? What independent corroboration was there for the miracles of the Old Testament?

The point could be pressed even further. What independent corroborating evidence is there for the miracles of the New Testament? We have the word of the books themselves. In some cases we also have the words of the early church fathers. But then, these fathers got their information from the New Testament. And so we seem to be back to square one. What we have before us are not the miracles of Jesus themselves but only *reports* of miracles. And there is a world of difference between seeing something for ourselves and merely reading a report of it.

Can There Be Violations of the Laws of Nature? But the really big objection to the biblical miracles does not turn on the amount of written evidence (or lack of it). It turns on the question of whether *any* evidence is admissable at all. It is not a matter of how many reports there are of any given miracle, but whether *any* testimony to the miraculous could be entertained by a modern, intelligent man or woman in his or her right mind. It is here that the argument against miracles by the seventeenth-century thinker Benedict de Spinoza comes in.

Spinoza's Argument. Spinoza was born into an immigrant Jewish family living in Holland. He was brought up in the Jewish faith, but was expelled from the synagogue for his unorthodox views.

Spinoza was impressed with the rationality of the world. But he went much further than any other rational philosopher of his day. He believed that reality was a single rational whole. He even went so far as to suggest that it be called either

"God" or "nature," depending on how you looked at it. He rejected the Jewish-Christian idea of God as the Creator. To him, there was no God over and above the world. Rational being itself was divine. The whole of nature was but the manifestation of a single rational being that people call God. In other words, Spinoza was a pantheist. But his pantheism was not that of the later Romantic poets who felt a divine oneness in everything. His system was all worked out like a series of theorems in geometry, supposedly on the basis of self-evident ideas.

Pantheistic systems have always foundered on two rocks. One is the problem of evil. If everything is a manifestation of God, then evil must also be a manifestation of God. But it is unthinkable to attribute evil to the character of God. The other rock is that of our own human autonomy. If everything is a manifestation of God, then all human thoughts and actions—every mistake, every lie, and every contradictory idea—must be a thought and action of God. Few people have found this credible, and Spinoza's philosophy as a total package has found few buyers. But his views on miracles—when detached from his system—appear more plausible. Spinoza set out his views on miracles in chapter 6 of his *Tractatus Theologico-Politicus* (1670).

The first big mistake people make, Spinoza argued, is to attribute to God anything that they do not understand. They imagine anything out of the ordinary to be the direct working of God. In other words, popular belief in miracles springs from ignorance of nature. But this mistake goes hand-in-hand with another. It is the assumption that God works only in the extraordinary. It leads people to look for God's working in the outlandish and the bizarre instead of the daily wonders of nature, which they just take for granted.

Underlying these errors, Spinoza argued, is the belief that God is like a capricious monarch, who every now and then gets it in his head to intervene in the normal course of events. But to Spinoza the laws of nature were divine decrees. They were perfect and simply could not be broken. To suggest that God broke his own decrees from time to time was unthinkable. It would be like suggesting that God was acting against his own nature, or that his wisdom needed correction.

The implications of Spinoza's argument were clear. Miracles, in the sense of violations of the laws of nature, were impossible. The things that people call miracles must be either stories about events that never really happened or instances of natural laws that have not yet been properly understood.

Spinoza went on to note hints and warnings in the Bible itself against undue fascination with signs and wonders and the misunderstanding of miracles. On the one hand, Deuteronomy 13 issued stern warnings against following miracle workers who themselves followed other gods. On the other hand, the Bible itself sometimes indicated the presence of natural causes. A case in point was the parting of the Red Sea, which was caused by a strong east wind blowing all night (Exodus 14:21). Spinoza even suggested that Jesus himself made use of natural means on at least one occasion in his healing work (John 9). Any event, he concluded, that is described in Scripture as having actually happened, must have done so like everything else in accordance with natural laws.

MORE QUESTION MARKS

Spinoza's argument was not exactly new. In fact, the question of miracles exercised the minds of people in the ancient world just as it does today. The Stoic philosophers said that God could do anything. But others were less ready to grant this. They claimed many things were impossible, even for God. Pliny declared that God could not change the past. He could not die. He could not give mortals immortality. He could not bring the dead back to life. He could not make twice ten unequal to twenty.

Other writers made similar points. What their writings show is that miracles were no easier to accept in the ancient world than they are today. When we talk about the ancient world, it is a mistake to think that everybody was alike. No doubt there were the credulous. Just as today in our technological world there is a market for astrology, fantastic tales of the supernatural, and sensational wonders, so in the ancient world there was a market for legends. But among the educated and many of the ordinary people there was a fine sense of what was possible and what was impossible. The very notion of a miracle is in itself an indication that it is unexpected. It is something people wonder at, precisely because it is contrary to the normal course of things.

Magic? For some people in the ancient world miracles just did not happen. Among them was the second-century philosopher Celsus. He was the author of the first major philosophical attack on Christianity. He called it *The True Word.* In it he argued that Jesus was really a magician who had picked up the tricks of his trade in Egypt. Celsus's book has long been lost. But most of it can be reconstructed from the reply of the church father Origen. His book *Against Celsus* responds to the philosopher's argument point by point. Origen met the charge of magic by drawing attention to the transforming power of Jesus in people's lives. Did magicians really free people from demons, restore people to health, and give them peace of mind? What sorcerer ever used his tricks to call his onlookers to moral reformation and educate them in the fear of God?

The charge of magic has been revived in our own day by Professor Morton Smith in his book *Jesus the Magician* (New York: Harper, 1978). It has not found wide acceptance. But it is worth looking at for the light it throws on the accounts of Jesus in the four Gospels. We shall get back to this question in Part II of this book.

What Do Miracles Prove? In the meantime a different sort of question mark was placed against miracles at the time of the Reformation. To be more exact, it is a question not so much of whether miracles could happen but of what precisely they proved. The question arose out of the battle between Catholics and Protestants. The Catholics argued that they were the true church because God was still working miracles among them. The miracles were like God's seal of approval. The Protestants were therefore wrong to split off from the Catholic Church. But the argument did not daunt Calvin. He replied by charging the Catholics with dishonesty. The Protestant church had miracles all right—the miracles in Scripture. They were "the seals of the gospel." Why then turn to another gospel? No amount of miracles should turn the believer away from the word of God in Scripture.

Quoting John 7:18 and 8:50 Calvin pointed out that true miracles bring glory to God. They have no other purpose than to glorify the name of God. But there are also Satanic signs and wonders that deceive those who refuse to love the truth (2 Thessalonians 2:9-10). There are signs and wonders performed by false prophets who seek to lead people astray after other gods (Deuteronomy 13). In short, the miraculous on its own was not for Calvin sufficient proof of God's activity. The true test of a miracle was whether it brought glory to God.

Calvin's point was well taken. But to many the argument was not quite so clear. Granted that the test of a true miracle was whether it brought glory to God, it was not at all clear that every claim to miracles after the Apostolic Age failed the test. Did not at least some Catholic claims to miraculous healings glorify God as well?

Growing Skepticism. In the eighteenth century, as the tide of skepticism grew stronger, people began to ask whether all the biblical miracles brought glory to God. The Deist Thomas Woolston recalled the stories about Apollonius of Tyana, who was reputed to have been a miracle worker living roughly the same time as Jesus. Commenting on the story of Jesus turning water into wine, Woolston declared, "If Apollonius Tyaneus, and not Jesus, had been the Author of this Miracle, we should have reproached his memory with it."

Few critics were as outspoken as Spinoza in the seventeenth century and Woolston in the eighteenth. But the tide was beginning to turn. Christians were becoming more and more defensive. The orthodox still believed in miracles. But they found themselves increasingly under attack. The appeal to miracles as divine seals of approval was no longer obvious and straightforward.

In fact, the theologians of the early church had already felt themselves under pressure on this score. As time wore on and the age of Jesus and the apostles receded increasingly into the past, the church fathers could no longer appeal to eyewitnesses of the original miracles. They themselves had only the reports of the Scriptures to go on. They continued to appeal to miracles. But they combined this with an appeal to prophecy. After all, if it could be shown that Jesus had fulfilled prophecies that had been made centuries earlier, there were fewer ifs and buts. One did not need to be an eyewitness. One simply needed to be sure that the prophecy was earlier than Jesus and that there were good grounds for thinking that Jesus had really fulfilled the prophecy.

Two Tracks of Argument. So there emerged two tracks of apologetic argument—miracles and fulfilled prophecy. From the time of Spinoza onward both tracks fell under increasingly heavy bombardment on the part of skeptics who did not believe in miracles and who thought that the prophecies either did not really fit Jesus or had been rigged in some way. The tough-minded among the orthodox continued to uphold the old arguments. But increasingly a shift of emphasis became apparent.

Some even inverted the old argument. The old argument went like this: "Since Jesus performed miracles, which only God could do, he must be divine." When inverted, the argument became: "Since Jesus is divine, he must have been capable of performing miracles." But in turning the argument upside down, miracles lost their place as a foundation for faith. Instead of being a foundation, they became the object of faith.

The liberals and radicals went even further. They wanted Jesus in some form, but wanted to dump the miracle stories altogether. They wanted religion, but religion without the encumbrances of what they considered to be the outworn legends and myths of earlier ages. In getting to that point, the miracle stories were not simply a cross to bear. They had become a cross to be dropped.

WHAT THEN SHOULD WE THINK ABOUT MIRACLES?

What should be our verdict? We are not yet in a position to give an answer. But it will help us to call on three witnesses.

The Witness of Augustine. The first of our three witnesses is Augustine (354-430), Bishop of Hippo in North Africa and the greatest theologian of the early church. In answer to the question "What is a miracle?" Augustine said that a miracle is "whatever appears that is difficult or unusual above the hope and power of them who wonder." Moreover, true miracles are not simply wonders that were designed to impress. They always met some human need, and in so doing revealed the graciousness of God.

Augustine actually anticipated Spinoza's objection that miracles were impossible because they were violations of the laws of nature. Augustine said that there was nothing wrong in saying "that God does a thing contrary to nature, when it is contrary to what we *know* of nature" (italics mine). In other words, a miracle is a miracle not because it violates anything. God never acts against his own nature. Miracles are what God does *with* nature. They may not be normal or common, but they are not contrary to God's divine order. They only violate what we know of God's order. Augustine even suggested that miracles might be instances of natural processes that were speeded up, or like seeds that lie dormant in nature until the time is right.

Why were miracles not more common? Augustine replied that nature is itself a continuous miracle. We just take it for granted. Familiarity breeds contempt. If the special events we call miracles were more common, we would take them for granted. God does not want us to love him simply because we are fascinated by the unusual. We need to be weaned from a love of the bizarre to the love of God for his own sake.

The Witness of Calvin. The second of our three witnesses is Calvin (1509-64). We have already heard him argue that miracles "seal" and "attest" the teaching of Scripture. But he also saw the miracles of Jesus and the apostles as sacramental signs. They illustrated and embodied the truth of the gospel. The term "sacrament" embraced for Calvin "all those signs which God has ever enjoined upon men to render them more certain and confident of the truth of his promises. He sometimes willed to present these in natural things, at other times set them forth in miracles." Just as the bread and the wine in the Lord's Supper attest and embody God's gracious promises, so the miracles attest and embody the grace of God.

The Witness of Luther. Our third and final witness is the great German Reformer Martin Luther (1483-1546). He too saw the miracles of Jesus as signs, accompanying and embodying the grace of God. They were tangible expressions of Jesus' teaching. The miracles were not direct revelations of what God is in himself. After all, in a miracle we do not actually *see* God in person. We see the *effects* of God's actions, just as we do in nature. To Luther miracles were like God's *masks* and *garments.*

> These are His masks or His garments, as it were, in which He conceals Himself. But He is certainly present in these, Himself working miracles, preaching, administering the sacraments, consoling, strengthening, and helping. We see Him as we see the sun through a cloud. (*Luther's Works* [St. Louis: Concordia, 1961], XXIV, 67)

But Luther made two other points that give us food for thought. On the one hand, he pointed out that God's ultimate victory was not a miracle of power. It was the cross. Satan and the powers of evil were defeated not by might or by a miracle of power but by Jesus' submission in weakness and death. For that reason, Luther could believe in miracles but nevertheless could say that miracles "are still the least significant works, since they are only physical and performed for only a few people." Christ's victory on the cross holds good for all God's children for all time.

On the other hand, Luther drew attention to a point that has frequently been lost from view. According to John 14:10-11, Jesus said:

> "Do you not believe that I am in the Father and the Father in me? The words that I say to you I do not speak on my own authority; but the Father who dwells in me does his works. Believe me that I am in the Father and the Father in me; or else believe me for the sake of the works themselves."

As Luther explained it, Christ is saying here:

> These are not only divine works, but they are also witnesses of God the Father. Therefore he who sees and hears these sees God the Father in them; and he is not only persuaded that God is in Christ and that Christ is in God, but from them he can also be comforted with the assurance of God's fatherly love and grace toward us.

In making this point, Luther is stressing the sacramental character of the miracles of Jesus. But he is also making a further point. The miracles of Jesus were not simply *his* miracles any more than the words of Jesus were simply *his* words.

They were not acts that he performed solely in his own right. They were the words and works of the Father.

Christian apologists have sometimes depicted miracles as violations of the order of nature. They have presented them as objective proof of God's activity and thus as God's seal of authentication. They have focused on the miracles of Jesus as evidence of his personal divinity and thus of the incarnation of the Son of God. In so doing, apologists have encountered the objections that we have come up against in this chapter.

Perhaps the time has come for us to listen more attentively to the witness of Augustine, Calvin, and Luther. If we do, we might find ourselves asking whether the traditional arguments are quite the right arguments. We might find ourselves asking whether we need to look beyond the apparent violations of nature to the harmony of a higher order, whether we need to look beyond the desire for objective proofs to the place of miracles in a sacramental universe, and whether we need to look at miracles not just in connection with the incarnation but rather in the context of the Trinity.

2 / David Hume and Company

> *A miracle is a violation of the laws of nature; and as a firm and unalterable experience has established these laws, the proof against a miracle, from the very nature of the fact, is as entire as any argument from experience can possibly be imagined.* (David Hume, *An Enquiry Concerning Human Understanding* [1748], Section 10, Part 1)

If Benedict Spinoza was the first in the field with his argument against miracles based on the laws of nature, David Hume's discussion of miracles is remembered today as the classic attack. Hume claimed to have hit upon his argument while talking with a Jesuit friend as he was walking one day in the cloisters of the Collège de la Flèche in Anjou, France.

He was no stranger to the Collège. Before he became famous as a writer and historian, the Scottish philosopher spent some years at the Flèche, where he quietly developed his ideas. At the time the Collège was a leading center of Catholic learning.

The Jesuit told Hume of a miracle that had occurred there. Hume replied that such a miracle was impossible. Taken aback, the Jesuit said that Hume's argument would work equally well against the miracles of Jesus in the Gospels. In reply Hume could only acknowledge that this was so. Moreover, his argument not only destroyed miracles. It also undermined the foundations of the case for Christianity. Or at least, Hume thought it did.

It was not until some years later that the celebrated argument appeared in print. Friends had counseled Hume not to publish it, and for a time he heeded their advice. But finally it appeared tucked in among his *Philosophical Essays Concerning Human Understanding* (later retitled *An Enquiry Concerning Human Understanding*). Some have found it odd that Hume's attack on miracles should find a place in such a work. But it was not at all odd to Hume. For Hume was discussing the questions "How do we know things?" "What in fact do we know?" "What can we know?" These questions affected religion just as much as they did everything else.

The Traditional Christian Answer. How do we know that the Christian faith is true? For years Catholics and Protestants had given much the same answer. Some things can be known by reason, but other things can be known only by revelation. The great English Empiricist philosopher John Locke was typical of his time. He drew a clear distinction between faith and reason. Reason enabled the mind to deduce truths from what we see, hear, touch, taste, and smell. Reason looks for evidence and sets about evaluating it. But faith gives assent to ideas that cannot be arrived at directly in this way. Faith, said Locke, has to do with revelation. Faith believes truths that can be known only by revelation.

It was reasonable, said Locke, to believe in the existence of God. Our minds can reflect on the order and signs of purpose in nature, and conclude that the universe was created by God. Such a belief was rational. But the Christian belief in the resurrection of the dead was above reason. How could we know this as a fact when all the people that we know to have died remain dead? The Christian answer to this question is: "Because it is revealed to us in Scripture that Christ will come again to judge the living and the dead at the general resurrection." But how do we know that this is so? How do we know that this is a revelation from God? It is at this point that miracles come in.

The answer Locke gave in books like *An Essay Concerning Human Understanding* (1690), *The Reasonableness of Christianity* (1695), and *A Discourse of Miracles* (1702) was typical of mainstream Christian thinking.

> To know that any revelation is from God, it is necessary to know that the messenger that delivers it is sent from God, and that cannot be known but by some credential given him by God himself.

Miracles and fulfilled prophecy provided just such credentials. To Locke a miracle was

> a sensible operation, which, being above the comprehension of the spectator, and in his opinion contrary to the established course of nature, is taken by him to be divine.

In short, miracles were like the credentials of an ambassador that authenticated his authority. Miracles were God's way of authenticating the Christian revelation in the Bible.

It was precisely this argument that David Hume tried to undermine in his discussion of miracles. If Hume could prove that miracles could not be proved, then the truth of Christianity could not be proved either.

HUME'S ARGUMENT

Hume's argument had two main parts. The first was general. It simply said that miracles were scientifically impossible. The second was more particular. It cast doubt on the kind of evidence put forward in support of miracles, and asked what miracles proved anyway.

The Scientific Impossibility of Miracles. The first part of Hume's argument amounted to a flat rejection of miracles.

> A miracle is a violation of the laws of nature; and as a firm and unalterable experience has established these laws, the proof against a miracle, from the very nature of the fact, is as entire as any argument from experience can possibly be imagined.

Christians were in the habit of appealing to experience. But so did modern eighteenth-century scientists, led by the greatest scientist of the age, Sir Isaac Newton. There were, however, important differences between the Christian appeal to experience and those made by the scientists of the day. The scientists made careful observations on the basis of controlled experiments. Christians did not. Moreover, the experiments of the scientists were repeatable and testable. The appeals of the Christians to experience were vague and general. In the case of the Christian appeal to miracles, the evidence was not there for anyone to inspect. It was all based on hearsay.

Hume knew full well that the laws of science were based on statistics. Some laws were better established than others, but the more science progressed, the more it became apparent that laws governed everything. Science left no room for the violation of the laws of nature.

Hume went on to argue that the Indian prince who refused to believe in ice "reasoned justly." He had no experience of water ever becoming solid. The notion of ice did not conform to his experience. He was therefore justified in refusing to believe in it.

Hume realized that experience was not infallible. But it was the best guide we have. A report of a miracle was more likely to be false than true. Science leads us to expect a natural explanation. Therefore, a miracle story must be either false or have a natural explanation. In either case it ceases to be a real miracle *in the sense of a violation of the laws of nature*. Hence, it is virtually impossible to prove the occurrence of a miracle on the basis of testimony.

The Credibility of the Witnesses. In the second part of his argument, Hume looked more closely at the kind of testimony put forward in favor of miracles. He made four observations.

First, Hume argued that no miracle in history has been attested by enough men of good sense, education and learning, integrity, and reputation to secure them against the charges of being either deluded themselves or out to deceive others. No miracle had been performed "in such a public manner and in so celebrated part of the world, as to render detection unavoidable." All these conditions were necessary in order to secure assurance in the testimony to miracles.

Secondly, Hume noted people's love to gossip and exaggerate. In villages and small towns two people of opposite sex can never see each other twice before the whole neighborhood has them paired off. People love to be the first with news. How often it happens that the news gets distorted. "Do not," Hume asked, "the same passions, and others still stronger, incline the generality of mankind to believe and report, with the greatest vehemence and assurance, all religious miracles?"

Thirdly, Hume remarked that miracles "are observed chiefly to abound among ignorant and barbarous nations." If "civilized people" admit them, it is not because they have seen a miracle for themselves. It is because they "have received them from ignorant and barbarous ancestors, who transmitted them with that inviolable sanction and authority, which always attend received opinions." Hume knew full well that many orthodox, intelligent, educated Christians in his own day believed in miracles. But it was not because they had seen anything of the sort themselves. It was because they happened to believe and revere the Bible, with its miracle stories set in rural Galilee and the like.

Finally, Hume argued that the miracle accounts of rival religions cancel each other out. If different religions all claim miracles, how can any of them prove its truth by appealing to miracles?

In all of this Hume studiously avoided mentioning the biblical miracles. But all the time he had in mind the arguments of Christian apologists. Instead of attacking the Gospel miracles head-on, Hume relentlessly sought to undermine their credibility and apologetic value.

At one point he discussed the Roman historian Tacitus's account of how the emperor Vespasian had cured a blind man by means of spittle and a lame man by the mere touch of his foot. With added irony Hume insisted that the event was "one of the best-attested miracles in all profane history." Echoing the arguments of Christian writers who were at pains to stress the integrity of the evangelists as historians, Hume made even stronger claims on behalf of Tacitus. Nevertheless, Hume was not prepared to believe him, precisely because miracles do not happen.

Turning to his own day Hume reflected on the widespread reported healings in Paris at the tomb of the recently deceased François de Pâris. François was a local saint who lived in a slum quarter. He died prematurely. From his funeral onward charismatic healings were reported in great numbers. The sensation rocked Paris. In the end the cemetery where François was buried was closed by royal decree. A wit put up a notice, "By order of the King, God is forbidden to perform miracles in this place."

Hume was well aware that the healings in Paris had been examined by doctors and men of repute and learning. They were just the sort of people who met his own criterion for competent witnesses. He admitted that the scene of the alleged events also fully met his requirements. But what had he to "oppose to such a cloud of witnesses, but the absolute impossibility or miraculous nature of the events which they relate? And this surely, in the eyes of all reasonable people, will alone be regarded as a sufficient refutation."

Hume's crowning example was to many people his most offensive. Suppose, he said, that Queen Elizabeth I had died on January 1, 1600. Her death had been ascertained by her physicians and the whole court. She had been buried a month. And then she had reappeared and governed England for three more years. Suppose, moreover, that all the historians were agreed on all this. What would Hume have to say?

He would say that her death had been pretended and that "it neither was, nor possibly could be real."

The point of the illustration could hardly have been misunderstood. It was a parody of the accounts of Christ's resurrection. No one familiar with the arguments of the Christian apologists could fail to see the parallels—not least Hume's stress on the impressive attestation of the alleged event. So far as Hume was concerned, no amount of attestation to such a miracle would suffice to overthrow his doubts.

With a final ironical flourish, Hume concluded that Christianity was founded on faith and not reason. No one could believe it without a miracle! "Mere reason is insufficient to convince us of its veracity: And whoever is moved by *Faith* to assent to it, is conscious of a continued miracle in his own person, which subverts all the principles of his understanding, and gives him a determination to believe what is most contrary to custom and experience."

. . . AND COMPANY

Of all the arguments against miracles, David Hume's is the most famous. It provoked replies in his own day, perhaps the most notable of which was George Campbell's *Dissertation on Miracles* (1762). But neither Hume nor Campbell said the last word on the subject. Hume's essay on miracles is still argued over by philosophers today. But it was not exactly original. The whole question of miracles had already been kicked around for a good many years. Moreover, Hume was careful to talk in generalities. Only at the beginning and at the end of his discussion did he mention Christianity directly. He avoided dealing with any specific miracle. He shunned discussion of details. His argument was all the more striking because he talked about principles and not specifics. But long before Hume came on the scene, the Deists had launched their onslaught on miracles. And some, at least, of the Deists had not been afraid to talk specifics.

The Deists' Attack on Miracles. In his celebrated *Dictionary of the English Language* Hume's contemporary, Dr. Samuel Johnson, defined a "Deist" as "a man who follows no particular religion, but only acknowledges the existence of God, without any other articles of faith." Most scholars date Deism from Lord Herbert of Cherbury. Lord Herbert was a man of many roles. For a time he served as the British ambassador in Paris. While in Paris he composed a work entitled *On Truth*, which was published in Latin in 1624. It argued for a rational, natural religion, independent of special revelation or particular creeds. The second edition of the book contained an attack on the Christian church.

Lord Herbert's disciple Charles Blount went still further. In 1680 he translated part of the *Life of Apollonius Tyaneus* by Philostratus. Apollonius was a reputed holy man of the first century whose activities bore some similarity to those of Jesus. If Apollonius could do miracles and other things like Jesus, the uniqueness of Jesus was considerably diminished. In 1683 Blount published a tract entitled *Miracles No Violations of the Laws of Nature.* The work was in fact a paraphrase of Spinoza's argument that we noted in the previous chapter.

The two most famous Deistic writings were John Toland's *Christianity Not Mysterious* (1696) and Matthew Tindal's *Christianity as Old as the Creation* (1730). Their authors argued for religion without revelation, for a form of Christianity without the church and the Bible. Clearly there was no real place for miracles in such a religion.

In the 1720s Anthony Collins attacked the idea of fulfilled prophecy. But it fell to former Cambridge scholar Thomas Woolston to launch an all-out attack on miracles. He did so in a series of six pamphlets that he called *Discourses on the Miracles of our Saviour.* Each was dedicated to a bishop of the Church of England. The tracts were filled with bitter ridicule. The star of Bethlehem was compared with a will-o'-the-wisp. Jesus' action in anointing the blind man in John 9 with clay and spittle "would sooner put a man's eyes out than restore a blind man to his sight." The resurrection of Jesus was a Robinson Crusoe romance, "the most self-evident imposture ever put upon the world."

In 1729 Woolston was tried for blasphemy. He was sentenced to a year's imprisonment and a fine of £100. He refused to retract or cease to write. He was still technically a prisoner when he died, despite the efforts of Samuel Clarke, the Anglican divine, and others to procure his release.

The Woolston case prompted Bishop Thomas Sherlock to write his own version of the affair. Sherlock was a kind of eighteenth-century C. S. Lewis. His book *The Tryal of the Witnesses of the Resurrection* (1729) was reprinted many times and became a minor classic in Britain and the Continent. Instead of putting Woolston on trial, Sherlock put the apostles in the dock. After detailed cross-examination the witnesses were acquitted and the resurrection pronounced to be a historical event.

Conyers Middleton's Attack on the Church Fathers. The Deistic controversy dragged on for several more years, but by the time Hume published his *Enquiry* it was virtually a thing of the past. The controversy over miracles, however, was still alive. It had been rekindled by Conyers Middleton's *Free Inquiry into the Miraculous Powers which are Supposed to have Subsisted in the Christian Church* (1748). Middleton was an Anglican scholar who was nearing the end of a stormy career. His book was a study of the history of alleged miracles in the early church.

Middleton began where the New Testament left off. He reviewed the writings of the church fathers and their testimony to continued miracles in the church. His work remains the most complete and the most destructive account of miracle stories in the early church. Although he dismissed the suggestion that his low view of the church fathers on the subject of miracles might also reflect adversely on the New

Testament, other people did not share that view. Middleton's outlook was much the same as Hume's. The same principles that Middleton applied to the fathers could equally be applied to the New Testament writers. John Wesley noted in his *Journal* that Middleton had contrived to "overthrow the whole Christian system." Wesley felt so strongly on the subject that he wrote a lengthy letter to Middleton, criticizing his book.

Middleton's book caused a sensation. For a time it overshadowed Hume's work. In his brief autobiography Hume told how he had returned from Italy in 1749 and experienced "the mortification to find all England in a ferment, on account of Dr. Middleton's *Free Inquiry*, while my performance was entirely overlooked and neglected."

Time has reversed this assessment of Hume's work. Still, Middleton's *Free Inquiry* remains a key work for anyone investigating healing miracles in the history of the church. B. B. Warfield drew heavily on Middleton in his own dismissal of miracles in the early church. In its own way Middleton's work contributed to the growing trend to secularize history. It influenced Edward Gibbon in his *Decline and Fall of the Roman Empire*. From this time onward historians looked increasingly for natural causes in history and dismissed the supernatural to the realm of legend, superstition, fraud, and pious wishful thinking. In his *Free Inquiry* Middleton spelled out the application of this secular approach and hard-headed thinking to early church history.

PROS AND CONS

What are we to make of Hume's argument? We can hardly deny that much of it appears to be very telling. We all know what Hume is talking about when he says that people love to gossip and exaggerate a bit. We all know sincere believers who seem incapable of admitting unpalatable facts.

Could it be that the miracle stories of the Bible were made up by just such people? Isn't it true that miracles always seem to be happening somewhere else? We never really see them for ourselves. Could not Hume be right when he insinuates that "miracles are observed chiefly to abound among ignorant and barbarous nations?" Isn't it more likely that miracle stories should be mistaken (for whatever reason) than that they should be true? Can we in our modern technological age really believe in miracles?

The strength and the weakness of Hume's whole case lie in the fact that Hume talks in generalities. The points he makes all contain obvious truths. But his argument works like a land mine. Because of the way it is set up, everything gets blown up, including Hume himself. There is no way in which Hume could carry his argument through consistently. In its individual parts Hume's argument is plausible, but it is full of internal contradictions and loose ends. To those familiar with Hume's philosophy as a whole there is also the question of whether his argument is consistent with his view of cause and effect.

At the outset of his discussion Hume laid down the principle that "a wise man . . . proportions his belief to the evidence." But he ends up by saying, in effect, that a wise man will refuse to look at the evidence at all. Or, if he does, he will just dismiss it. Once he has made up his mind that a miracle is "a violation of the laws of nature," Hume allows nothing to count as such a violation. Whatever evidence there might be is automatically dismissed.

Hume claims too much when he says that "a firm and unalterable experience has established" the laws of nature. It raises the question, "Whose experience?" For all his display of desire for open, honest investigation, Hume gives the impression of having closed his mind to anything that would upset his view of things.

A further difficulty calls in question Hume's entire position. A major feature of Hume's philosophy was his discussion of the nature of cause and effect. Hume claimed that the whole notion of cause and effect was something that "we *feel* in the mind." It is a product of the "imagination." It is based on our experience of the conjunction of objects. But beyond that Hume believed that "no objects have any discoverable connexion together."

Hume's views have given rise to a discussion among philosophers as to whether, if taken seriously, they would undermine the whole foundation of natural science and indeed of everyday living. Did Hume think that cause and effect were purely subjective ideas without any objective reality in the physical world? If so, he had no right to talk about "laws of nature." For the very idea of law presupposes relations of cause and effect. Moreover, he had no right to dismiss miracles in the name of the laws of nature. For without cause and effect no laws can be violated. There can only be habits of expectation that Hume professes himself unable to break.

Hume's comments about the nature of evidence are also too wholesale. It is conceivable that they might apply in general to this or that reputed miracle. But like any general rule, the question remains whether they apply to this or that particular case.

Hume insisted that no miracle had been attested by enough men of learning, education, reputation, etc. in "so celebrated part of the world" as to render detection of misrepresentation or fraud unavoidable. If such criteria were generally applied, the only history that could have been written at all would be that concerning the metropolitan centers of Europe from about the fifteenth century onward. The only people whose views on anything would count would be those who shared Hume's intellectual outlook. As Hume's argument unfolded, he made it clear that he discounted the testimony of his educated contemporaries when it contradicted his own experience.

Hume's second observation was equally wholesale. It tacitly assumed that all who bore witness to miracles were prone to gossip and exaggeration. No doubt some people are. But a rigorous historian needs to be more precise. He does not simply write off testimony to the unusual on the assumption that all people who relate such stuff are simpleminded liars, gossips, or credulous fools. Like a detective, the careful historian tries to find out what sort of witness relates the testimony. If the man or woman who tells of a miracle is naturally simpleminded, etc., we may be inclined to think that Hume was right. But if the witness was a skeptic to start with and then changed his or her mind because of what he or she saw, Hume's argument loses its sting.

Hume's third observation about miracle stories—that they "are observed chiefly to abound among ignorant and barbarous nations"—has a certain ring of plausibility. But it sets aside without argument reports of contemporary healing and earlier reports of miracles in identifiable centers of civilization. Moreover, the implication of the observation is arbitrary. For it contains the tacit demand that miracles should occur in places of Hume's own choosing.

Hume's fourth observation—that the miracles of rival religions would cancel each other out—is plausible but specious. The argument would work if rival religions had identical miracles supporting contradictory claims. But we do not find Islam, Judaism, Buddhism, and Christianity all claiming to have a Christ who has been raised from the dead and who thereby is shown to be the Son of God. Of all the religions in the world only Christianity makes this claim.

It is true that claims to miraculous healing are made by different religions and, indeed, by rival groups within Christianity. But Christianity claims no monopoly on the gift of healing. Nor, in fact, can it claim to have a monopoly on miracles. Nurses and doctors bring healing to people regardless of the creed of the patient or the healer. Only the sectarian mentality supposes that it alone has a monopoly. Through the ages the Christian church has taught that God has no favorites. It is not because of what we are or do that God lavishes his goodness on us. As Jesus said, the Father "makes his sun to shine on the evil and on the good, and sends his rain on the just and the unjust" (Matthew 5:45). The gift of healing is no monopoly of any religion or any sect within a religion. Where healing occurs, it is what the theologians call "common grace." And this applies to "faith healing" just as much as to healing through doctors, nurses, drugs, surgery, and hospitals.

Suppose that someone asks, "But what about the miracles of Jesus?" "Was there nothing special about them?" "Do you mean to say that Jesus was just an ordinary healer?" I am going to give my full answer in Chapters 10–12. In the meantime I will say just this. Jesus' healings were special, not because he healed when nobody else could (though this was also true). What was special about Jesus' miracles was that they were the works of the Kingdom of God. They were the special work of God that brought glory to God. They were not just any healings but the works of the Christ, foretold in prophecy and fulfilled by Jesus.

THREE OBSERVATIONS

Before we leave David Hume and company, three more observations must be made.

Testimony. First, we must note that Hume's argument has to do largely with testimony. He was conducting a kind of cross-examination of verbal witness reports. But his argument leaves untouched evidence of a more general kind. I will leave until later the details of my case. But I think that two areas of argument emerge unscathed from Hume's criticisms. One of these (and many scholars have argued the point) is the resurrection of Jesus. Belief in Jesus' resurrection does not depend simply upon the accuracy of individual testimony reported in the Gospels. It also depends on the very existence of the church. Without the resurrection of Jesus the existence of the church is unthinkable. For the whole basis of the church's existence is the belief, confirmed by experience, that

God raised him from the dead. My other argument turns on a point that has largely passed unnoticed. It has to do with the fact that not just Christians but the Jewish leaders of his day perceived Jesus as a worker of signs and wonders. But of this, more later.

A Question of Definition. Our second observation has to do with Hume's definition of miracles. He defined a miracle as "a violation of the laws of nature." But what about those miracles in which God *controls* nature? Hume leaves these out completely. We shall look at them more closely in Chapter 6.

What Do We Expect? We may put our third and final observation in the form of a question. "What does Hume expect a miracle to be?" "What, in fact, do we expect a miracle to be?" Hume actually gave two definitions. In the first, he said simply that "A miracle is a violation of the laws of nature." In his second definition Hume added a further qualification. He wrote: "A miracle may be accurately defined, *a transgression of a law of nature by a particular volition of the Deity, or by the interposition of some invisible agent.*" Even if we stick (for the purposes of argument) with the view that a miracle transgresses the laws of nature, all that Hume has done is to give a definition of a miracle and not a refutation of the possibility of miracles.

　　Granted that miracles are improbable. Granted that we would not expect them to happen. If they were not improbable or unexpected, they would not be miracles—they would just be ordinary events. By introducing into his definition the question of agency (the part of God or some invisible agent, e.g., an angel), what Hume has done is to define the truth-conditions for an event to qualify as a miracle. Ordinary events are capable of being explained without bringing God into the explanation. What distinguishes a miracle from an ordinary event is the special part God plays in it.

In one sense, of course, everything is a miracle. Sunrise and sunset. The passage of the seasons. The blooming of flowers and fruit from tiny shriveled seeds. The gift of life. All these things—and countless more—are miracles. They are miracles in the sense that we simply would not believe them if we had never seen them before. Because they are so common, we lose our sense of wonder. In a sense, all nature is miraculous. It is because there is so much of nature, and because nature keeps on repeating herself, that we stop seeing any miracles in her. But what about these special events that we call miracles?

Left to her own devices, we would expect nature to behave normally. Nature could not do anything other than that. But if God is God, and if God is the author of nature, then occasionally—when it suits his purpose—we might have to reckon with God's doing things that we had never seen before.

3 / The Curious Case of the King of Siam

"Hitherto I have believed the strange things you have told me, because I look upon you as a sober fair man; but now I am sure you lie." (The King of Siam to the Dutch ambassador in John Locke, *An Essay Concerning Human Understanding* [1690], Book 4, Chapter 15)

David Hume has told us the story of the Indian prince who refused to believe in ice. But Hume did not invent him. He was alive and well some sixty years earlier when he appears in John Locke's story of the King of Siam. The King, so the story goes, was being entertained by the Dutch ambassador. He was fascinated by the tales the ambassador told about his far-off country. And then the ambassador told him that sometimes in his country, in cold weather, water could become so hard that people, even an elephant, could walk on it. To this the King replied, "Hitherto I have believed the strange things you have told me, because I look upon you as a sober fair man; but now I am sure you lie."

The argument has fascinated generations of philosophers. The King of Siam (alias the Indian prince) turns up again in the writings of Bishop Sherlock, Bishop Butler, and David Hume in the eighteenth century and J. S. Mill in the nineteenth. Was the King right to doubt? Hume thought that he was. After all, the King had never seen ice in his life. He had never lived outside a tropical climate. There were no refrigerators in the seventeenth century. To Hume skepticism was the safest and wisest course. He believed in sticking to what you knew and letting experience decide.

USES AND ABUSES OF ANALOGY

In a curious way Locke's story pinpoints the problem of miracles. It embodies what philosophers call the principle of analogy. The word "analogy" denotes a likeness or similarity. It suggests a resemblance between things. In an analogy one thing is like another. When I see two things that look like each other, I can identify their common characteristics. This in turn enables me to recognize the same characteristics in other things.

Analogy and Daily Life. Life is based on analogy. When I turn on the light switch, I expect the light to come on. Why? Because of my past experience. I have turned on so many light switches in the past that I expect lights to come on in the future when I perform the same action again. If they do not, I suspect that the light bulb is not working, or that the wires are not connected, or a power failure. Why? Because one or more of these causes have been the reason why lights have not come on in the past when I have turned on switches. In other words, I am using analogy. Experience in the past is my guide to the present and future.

We use analogy in every department of life. The doctor uses analogy to help in diagnosis. The appearance of distinct red circular spots on the skin suggests another case of measles. The onset of a low-grade fever and the formation of vesicles indicate a case of chicken pox.

We talk about someone's track record—not only in sports. The track record of the politician in office plays a part in determining whether we will vote for him or her again. The track records of the rival candidates help us to decide whether we prefer them instead.

In a sense, education is really about analogy. It has to do with helping us to recognize things for what they are. It is about learning to discern what things are like and what things are unlike. For there are limits to analogy. Education helps us to learn to discern where analogy applies and where it does not apply.

Damon Runyon once remarked that "The race is not always to the swift, nor the battle to the strong, but that's the way to bet." The safe way to bet is to use analogy. But the use of analogy in betting is not foolproof. To the detached observer, analogy suggests that it is best not to bet at all.

BACK TO THE QUESTION OF MIRACLES

In refusing to believe the Dutch ambassador the King of Siam was using analogy. After all, facts were facts. He had a lifetime's experience to go on. Whoever in the tropics in the seventeenth century had ever heard of water becoming solid, let alone so solid that an elephant could walk on it? And yet he was wrong.

In the hindsight of our experience, we can say "How stupid!" The King was using his limited experience to lay down what was possible. And yet he had only the word of the ambassador to tell him otherwise. We have to use our limited experience and understanding as our guide in life. And yet if we stay put and refuse to entertain anything new, we shall never learn anything. If anything new comes our way, we shall simply turn a blind eye to it. In a funny sort of way, we shall be like modern flat-earthers. We shall steadfastly shut our minds to anything that conflicts with our preconceived ideas, and resolutely endeavor to explain everything in terms of our limited vision.

Analogy and Our View of Reality. C. S. Lewis tells the story of the determined agnostic who found himself in the Lake of Fire at the end of the world. He doggedly continued to regard his experiences there as an illusion, looking for explanations from psychoanalysis and cerebral pathology.

What was Lewis's agnostic really doing? He was building his worldview on the analogies and interpretations that he had come to accept, and was refusing to allow anything to shake them. No matter what the experience was, his worldview was fixed. Nothing was allowed to challenge it. Nothing could modify it. The agnostic had constructed for himself a frame of reference based on a rigid set of interpretations. So far as he could, he interpreted everything that came his way by analogy with that frame of reference. If there was no analogy at hand that could provide an explanation, he promptly dismissed the new experience as an illusion.

In the nineteenth century the great German philosopher and theologian Ernst Troeltsch laid down the principle that analogy was the key to historical understanding. When the historian looks at a document and reads a story, how does he decide whether it is true? He may have only the one account. He has to ask whether it fits other items of information he already accepts. But even it if does, there may be parts of the story that have to be judged on their own merits. What then? The historian asks himself how the account reads in the light of his own experience and understanding. Does it ring true? In other words, he is using analogy with his own experience and understanding to determine the truth of a report.

Analogies for the Resurrection? The historian knows that dragons and unicorns do not exist. There are no such creatures in the animal world. So if the historian reads an account of Saint George killing a dragon in order to rescue a fair maiden, he knows that it is myth or legend. But what about the story of a man being raised from the dead? There are no analogies between our experience and such an event. This is why modern theologians like Rudolf Bultmann and Paul Tillich regard the resurrection narrative in the Gospels as mythical. The restoration of life to a dead man does not fit their view of the world. It bears no analogy to their experience and understanding of the physical world.

One scholar who says that they were wrong is Wolfhart

Pannenberg. He argues that the resurrection of Jesus is an event that bursts all analogies with our present experience. But there are still good grounds for thinking that it was an event in history. For the very existence of the church cannot be explained without presupposing the resurrection of Christ.

Jesus was publicly tried and condemned for blasphemy. At the time of his execution his followers were in complete disarray. Yet shortly afterward they began to preach that God had raised Jesus up. They faced continued persecution and hardship for their beliefs. It would have been easy to have given up. If it was all lies and fabrication, there would have been no point in carrying on. And yet their faith was centered on the risen Christ and his teaching. Everything was so bound up with the resurrection of Jesus that the most rational explanation of the emergence of the church is the presupposition of the resurrection as a historical event.

The resurrection of Jesus is an event that bursts all our analogies based on our present experience. It calls in question our understanding of what is possible. If we are confronted with something that we do not understand—something that we would have said was impossible—we have two courses of action. One course is to go on doubting. We can go on suspecting that there is something wrong somewhere. Either it did not happen or there is a natural explanation that we don't know of. The other course is to question our previous assumptions. Maybe our world is too small. Maybe our present experience should not fool us into imagining that we know everything there is to know.

Analogy and Miracles. Of course, miracles are improbable. They would not be miracles if they were not improbable. Of course, we cannot predict them in the same way the scientist predicts things on the basis of proven experiments. That is what makes them miracles. If they were common, repeatable events that could be reproduced on demand, they would simply be ordinary events.

Miracles are like warning flags. They signal the presence of a different order of reality that is present in the midst of our everyday world. David Hume thought of miracles as violations of the laws of nature. But there is another way of thinking about them. It is to see them not so much as violations of an existing order but as indications of the presence of a different order. On this view, miracles are not bizarre, random events. They are tokens of a higher order that is ultimately more real than our world of change and decay. They are sacramental signs of gracious love. Like the bread and the wine in the sacrament of the Lord's Supper, they pass away. But the gracious love remains.

Not every miracle story is such a sacramental sign. Some are fakes. Others rest on little more than pious sentiment. To open the door to the possibility of miracles is not to open the door to every myth and legend. But how do we know the difference between the genuine and the fake? Once more we are back with the question of analogy.

The Christian believer also uses analogy. David Hume and company had no monopoly on the use of analogy. But the kind of question that David Hume and the King of Siam asked was limited. They asked, in effect, "Does the miracle story bear any analogy to my understanding of nature?" It is not surprising that they get the answer "No!" But the kind of question that the believer asks is broader. It asks: "Does the miracle story bear any analogy to my understanding of God and his creation?" It does not prejudge the issue. It does not mean that in order to believe in miracles we have to abandon all our scientific understanding. It recognizes that science is competent to deal with those things that fall within its scope. But things that fall outside the scope of science are a different matter.

The believer's question gives recognition to the fact that scientific credibility is not the only kind of credibility at issue. There is also the matter of theological credibility. It is no less important to ask, "Does the miracle story fit what we know of the character of God?" That is why the Book of Deuteronomy gave the Israelites the instruction:

> "If a prophet arises among you, or a dreamer of dreams, and gives you a sign or a wonder, and the sign or wonder which he tells you comes to pass, and if he says 'Let us go after other gods,' which you have not known, 'and let us serve them,' you shall not listen to the words of that prophet or to that dreamer of dreams; for the LORD your God is testing you, to know whether you love the LORD your God with all your heart and with all your soul. You shall walk after the LORD your God and fear him, and keep his commandments and obey his voice, and you shall serve him and cleave to him." (Deuteronomy 13:1-4)

In other words, truth demands that we look for analogies not only with our understanding of nature but with God's revelation of himself. The Christian operates with two frames of reference. One is our understanding of the natural world. The other is our understanding of God.

TWO OBSERVATIONS

Before we leave this subject two further observations must be made.

Miracles and Belief in God. The first is that miracles do not normally serve to establish belief in God. In some cases they may tip the scales. The experience of a miracle may cause us to swing from agnosticism or superstition to an acknowledgment of God as a loving, caring person. But generally accounts of miracles come to people who have an already established framework of belief. To them the miracle serves not to prove the existence of God but to bring home a new glimpse of his character. It tells them something fresh about the God they knew already in a partial sort of way.

A Two-Way Process. The second observation is that analogy is really a two-way process. We use our present understanding to assess reports that come to us from the past. But we also use the past to enable us to understand the present and to face the future.

The believer does both these things quite apart from miracles. When we read stories about battles, murder, passion, love, and kindness, we understand what they are about because we know something about these things from our own experience. We are using the present to interpret the past. But when we read, say, the Twenty-third Psalm, "The LORD is my shepherd, I shall not want," we are reading about the Psalmist's testimony. We are interested in it not only for what it tells us about the Psalmist, but for what it tells us about God and ourselves. When we recite this Psalm—or any other Psalm—we are identifying ourselves with the Psalmist and his situation. And whether we recognize it or not, we are applying the principle of analogy. If God was like that for the Psalmist then, he will be like that for us today.

When Jesus performed miracles, his actions had a significance beyond the immediate act of healing. His actions were signs of the Kingdom of God. They were indications of a higher order breaking into our natural order. His healings were a sign that God is the ultimate healer. His control over nature was a sign of God's control over nature. His resurrection was the firstfruits of the new order of resurrection life. And in all these things God was in Christ, drawing our attention to who he was and pointing us to the future.

If we fail to find analogies between the miracles of Jesus and our present understanding of the way things are, it may be that we are facing in the wrong direction. It may be that we are like the King of Siam. We may be using the present to judge the past, when what we need to do is to allow the past to judge the present and open us to God's future.

4 / C. S. Lewis to the Rescue—
Well Almost

Experience by itself proves nothing. If a man doubts whether he is waking, no experiment can solve his doubt, since every experiment may itself be part of the dream. Experience proves this, or that, or nothing according to the preconceptions we bring to it. (C. S. Lewis, *God in the Dock* [Grand Rapids: Eerdmans, 1970], pp. 25-26)

Few Christian writers have made a greater impact than C. S. Lewis. As an Oxford don and later as a Cambridge professor, Lewis taught English literature as a profession. But on the side he poured out a steady stream of Christian books. Lewis's writings have delighted and inspired millions of readers. They have also earned him a reputation as a giant killer, a modern David, ready to take on all comers and come out on top.

C. S. Lewis had a unique gift for speaking common sense. He was not afraid to appear unfashionable. In an age of skepticism he was a believer. In an academic world that sneered at the age-old beliefs of the Christian church he stood up for orthodoxy. With a quiet, polished humor he burst the bubbles of specious arguments and tore to shreds the fashionable assumptions of skeptics both inside and outside the church. Lewis had a way of putting things in a new light. He breathed sanity, spirituality, and sense into acrimonious debate. At a time when church leaders fell back into meaningless platitudes, C. S. Lewis, the lay theologian, spoke up for his beliefs. And if those beliefs seemed old-fashioned to some,

Lewis lost no sleep over it. Fashion, after all, is for those who have not discovered who they really are. C. S. Lewis had found himself by losing himself in Christ. He dedicated his life to explaining the truth of God in Christ to a generation that was eager to hear what he had to say.

In 1942, when Britain was struggling for survival in the horrors of World War II, C. S. Lewis published a book that wrestled with the problem of evil. He called it *The Screwtape Letters*. It purported to contain letters from a senior to a junior devil, outlining a plan of campaign to ensnare a victim. The book became a classic piece of popular apologetics, giving a new credibility to the traditional view of the conflict between God and the powers of evil. In the same year Lewis delivered a sermon on a subject that seemed equally unpromising to the skeptical minds of his day. Its subject was "Miracles," and it was later reprinted in *God in the Dock*. The sermon turned out to be a kind of trial run for Lewis's discussion of the same theme in his best-seller *Miracles: A Preliminary Study* (1947). What Lewis did for the problem of evil in *The Screwtape Letters* he now did for the New Testament miracles. To the modern skeptical mind, devils and miracles both belong to the outworn mythical beliefs of antiquity. What Lewis did was to make them credible.

A QUESTION OF APPROACH

Preconceptions. To Lewis the problem was not the amount (or lack) of evidence there may (or may not be) for any given miracle. The real problem lies in the way we look at things. Seeing is not believing, for what we see is regularly colored by our existing deep-seated beliefs. Not only religious believers do this. The atheist and the agnostic do it as well. Lewis suggested that if the end of the world appeared with all the literal trappings described in the Book of Revelation, and the modern materialist saw with his own eyes the heavens rolled up and the great white throne appearing, and if he had the sensation of being hurled into the Lake of Fire, the materialist would put it all down to an illusion and look for an explanation in psychoanalysis or cerebral pathology.

Lewis's Strategy. The same argument applies to miracles. Whatever the evidence might be, the materialist would explain it away. For Lewis, therefore, the main problem was to clear the ground. Misconceptions had to be cleared away and a worldview established in which miracles could be seen to have a real place. For this reason C. S. Lewis devoted three-quarters of his book to developing a view of God and the world in general. Only in the closing chapters does Lewis discuss miracles in particular. The result was a book that outlined Lewis's philosophy of religion and in turn provided a framework for Lewis's understanding of miracles.

As an educated, intelligent modern man, Lewis had no desire to revert to a prescientific worldview. He would have nothing to do with the idea that some events happened naturally while others were purely supernatural. Miracles could only be properly appreciated against the background of the normal workings of nature. If there were no ordered regularities in nature, nothing would distinguish a miracle from all other random events. On the other hand, belief in miracles requires belief in some reality beyond nature. Otherwise, the events that we call miracles would simply be random quirks, unusual happenings, and occurrences that came about naturally but as yet lacked a natural explanation.

AN INTERFERENCE WITH NATURE

Lewis's Definition of a Miracle. To C. S. Lewis, miracles were not what they were to David Hume—violations of the laws of nature (which as such would be impossible). Rather, Lewis preferred to think of a miracle as "an interference with Nature by supernatural power" (*Miracles,* p. 15). A miracle did not simply set aside nature. Nor did it break any laws of nature. Once God had initiated the miracle, nature took over again. If God chose to create a miraculous spermatozoon in the body of the virgin Mary, he did not proceed to break the normal subsequent laws of pregnancy. Pregnancy followed conception, and a child was born nine months later. The miracle lay in the divine initiative in altering some part of God's created order. Once the initiative has been taken the rest follows naturally.

Miracles and Order. To Lewis the divine ordering of nature that we call miraculous was not unlike our human ordering of nature, which occurs on a much less grand scale. Lewis was a confirmed pipe smoker. He observed that when he knocked out his pipe, he was altering the position of a great many atoms. But nature was able to digest and assimilate the event with ease and harmonize it with all other events. In performing the action, he was not breaking any natural law. But he was interfering with the position of the atoms of tobacco ash in his pipe. To Lewis the action was a reflection of the way in which God, as a personal being, interacts with the world. He does not violate the order that he has created, but arranges their patterns and determines what sequence of events should be initiated and what should not. In doing this, God sometimes makes use of the existing natural laws of the present world. But sometimes he also makes use of the order of the world to come.

I shall come back to this point in a moment. But before I do so, it is important to note that Lewis would have nothing to do with the suggestion that belief in miracles is aided by appealing to the principle of indeterminacy in modern physics. Lewis felt the need to express great caution as to what might be inferred from this theory. As a layman in the field of science, he could not help wondering whether physicists actually mean to say that nature is really random and lawless at a subatomic level or whether it was a matter of our inability to observe and predict the position of particles. In any case, Lewis did not want to attribute miracles to random flukes of nature. He believed in an ordered universe that was open to the personal action of human beings and of God.

The Difficulty with Materialism. Writing against the background of scientific materialism, Lewis saw it as his main task to show the difficulties of materialism and the cogency of belief in a transcendent, personal God. The materialist believes that there is nothing but matter. Everything happens of its own accord. Even our thinking is determined by physical factors over which we have no control. But Lewis found this kind of deterministic materialism to be self-refuting. He endorsed the view of the British scientist J. B. S. Haldane:

> If my mental processes are determined wholly by the motions of atoms in my brain, I have no reason to suppose that my beliefs are true . . . and hence I have no reason for supposing my brain to be composed of atoms. (*Miracles,* pp. 28-29)

The alternative was to presuppose that the human mind was more than a collection of atoms. In a sense it was "supernatural." This thought in turn led to the idea that there is a "cosmic mind" that is not the product of mindless nature. Rather, nature itself is a product of the "cosmic mind." And to admit this sort of "cosmic mind" is to admit a God outside nature, a transcendent and supernatural God.

In making this point, Lewis felt rather like Julius Caesar when he reached the Rubicon. If he remained on the bank, he would be safe but he could not win. If he crossed the river and burned his boats, there could be no going back. He had to be ready for anything. Lewis believed that it was the same with God. If we are prepared to reckon with the reality of God, we have to be prepared to reckon with the possibility of God's interference with his world. We have to be prepared to reckon with miracles.

At this point Lewis made a running jump. He jumped

from a natural theology to a biblical theology. On the bank behind him lay his natural theology with its critique of naturalism based on general philosophical considerations and its affirmation of a supernatural cosmic mind. On the bank on which he now stood he proceeded to develop a theological rationale of the Gospel miracles, inspired by the fourth-century bishop and theologian Athanasius and the Victorian preacher and writer George MacDonald. It was they who supplied him with the key to his understanding of the point of the miracle stories.

MIRACLES OF THE OLD CREATION

Lewis saw a parallel between miracles and God's acts in general. What God incarnate did as a man living in Palestine is a small-scale counterpart to what God does generally. His actions focus at a particular point on what God does now in a general way, or will do in the future. When they focus on what God does now in a general way in the world, they may be called Miracles of the Old Creation. When they focus on what God will do in the future, they may be called Miracles of the New Creation.

Lewis found justification for his view in the pronouncement of John 5:19: " 'The Son can do nothing of his own accord, but only what he sees the Father doing.' " The key to it all was the "grand miracle" of the incarnation. Lewis went on to see cases of Miracles of the Old Creation in the healing miracles of Jesus, the miracle at Cana in turning water into wine, and the feeding of the five thousand. Healing goes on every day. But in the healing stories the healing is focused in the action of Jesus. God was doing through him what he does at large generally.

God is continually turning water into wine—but through the natural processes of nature in which rain produces the growth of grapes and grape juice is fermented into wine. Fish are multiplied daily in ponds, rivers, lakes, and seas. Likewise grain multiplies in the fields from seed. These are all natural miracles. In the New Testament stories Lewis revived an idea found in Augustine and other church fathers. He saw in these miracles a concentration of divine activity that performed in an instant what nature can perform only over a prolonged period.

MIRACLES OF THE NEW CREATION

But the Miracles of the New Creation are different. Nature has no parallels to them at all. The resurrection of Jesus was not like the raising of Jairus's daughter or the resuscitation of Lazarus. Jairus's daughter and Lazarus were restored to what they were before. But the resurrection of Jesus was not simply his restoration to physical life. His resurrection body was a transformed, glorified body. It represents the breaking into our old order of the new order. For this reason C. S. Lewis saw the resurrection of Jesus as a Miracle of the New Creation. It was not simply a random event. Nor was it a violation of the order of nature. It was the firstfruits of the new order breaking into our present world.

In Roman Catholic circles there is a saying about Thomas Aquinas: "Thomas has spoken; the case is closed." In some evangelical circles today the impression is given that when C. S. Lewis has said anything, nothing much remains to be said. But has Lewis said the last word on miracles? Has he rescued belief in miracles once and for all? Lewis himself was more modest in his claims than some of his posthumous admirers. He deliberately called his book on miracles *A Preliminary Study*. It was more an exploratory essay than a definitive statement. It was a semipopular book written for general readers and not a technical study that met professional philosophers and theologians on their own ground.

LEWIS'S ARGUMENT REVISITED

Strengths. As I read Lewis's work today, I am struck by his insights but also by some fundamental flaws in the structure of his argument. On the credit side, I think that Lewis was wise not to get entangled in speculation about the theological implications of indeterminacy in nuclear physics. Here his instincts were right. Theologians and apologists can easily get out of their element in trying to draw implications from technical disciplines outside their expertise. Lewis rightly saw that no mileage could be gotten from trying to explain miracles by appealing to the concept of indeterminacy. Miracles are not made plausible by arguing that nature is at its heart disorderly. Miracles can appear as miracles only in the light of the ordering of nature.

Lewis made a further important point in arguing that a miracle should not be thought of as a violation but as "an interference with Nature by supernatural power." He rightly saw that the key factor lies in what we have earlier called our frame of reference (see Chapter 3). If we are materialistic determinists, nothing can be allowed to count as evidence for a miracle, for we shall see everything within a materialistic, deterministic frame of reference. Inevitably we shall attempt to give everything an explanation in terms of natural, physical causes. Lewis devoted a great deal of energy to showing the inadequacies of materialistic determinism. Lewis showed that this view failed to do justice to the concept of mind and our experience of ourselves as moral, personal beings. His arguments were in fact much the same as those of his contemporaries A. E. Taylor, William Temple, and H. H. Farmer. Lewis was not an original thinker on this score. But he had a unique ability to express abstract ideas in a graphic, cogent, and even witty way.

Weaknesses. Lewis's argument was not, however, without flaws. Even if we grant that Lewis made a good case for belief in a "cosmic mind" and go on to admit a transcendent, personal God outside nature, it does not follow that such a transcendent, personal God must necessarily be the God described in the Bible or even a miracle-working God at all. In fact, the

English Deists (whom we looked at in Chapter 2) professed belief in precisely such a transcendent God and felt no need at all to go on to believe in miracles or special interventions by such a God. It requires a leap of faith to jump from a "cosmic mind" to the miracle-working God of the New Testament.

Jewish believers have faith in a transcendent Yahweh, but they find in their faith no grounds for going on to believe in the miracles of Jesus as works of Yahweh. Indeed, it is precisely the theology that supplies their frame of reference that deters them from accepting Christian claims. Despite his many insights and incisive attacks on materialistic determinism, Lewis's philosophical theology fails to provide compelling reasons for belief in a miracle-working God. His natural theology points him to a transcendent, personal God; his biblical theology points him to a miracle-working God. He gets from one to the other by a leap of faith.

When we turn to Lewis's biblical theology, there are things that are suggestive but also things that beg questions. How far can we press the parallel between God's actions in Christ and God's actions generally? In a general sense we can say that the actions of Jesus are also the actions of the Father. We shall have more to say about this later on. But it does not really help us if we were to claim that the changing of water into wine and the feeding of the five thousand were really only accelerated instances of natural processes. It is one thing for grapes to be gathered and their juice fermented and bottled. It is another thing for water to become wine without the aid of vines and all the subsequent processing. It is one thing for fish to multiply in the sea and grain to multiply in the fields. It is another thing to suggest that dead fish multiply on dry land and grain becomes more grain and is changed into bread without all the intermediate stages. In any case, the acceleration theory still leaves us with a miracle beyond human explanation.

But Lewis's idea of Miracles of the New Creation deserves closer attention. To the apostle Paul, the resurrection of Christ was not an absolutely unique event. In one sense, it was of course unique. Christ was unique, and his resurrection was unprecedented. But in another sense Paul could describe it as the prototype of the general resurrection of Christ's people (1 Corinthians 15). His resurrection is the ground of our hope.

C. S. Lewis had good theological reasons for seeing the resurrection of Jesus as a Miracle of the New Creation. But perhaps some of the other miracles in the Gospels are better seen, not as Miracles of the Old Creation, but as anticipations of God's new order breaking into our order. Perhaps we should see the feeding of the five thousand as an anticipation of the messianic banquet. Perhaps C. S. Lewis could be faulted for not fully grasping important theological points and for not seeing the dynamics of what was described in the Gospels. But he certainly left behind him important clues, and it is now up to his successors to follow them up.

5 / What Sort of World Do We Live In?

In my view the biosphere is unpredictable for the very same reason—neither more nor less—that the particular configuration of atoms constituting this pebble I have in my hand is unpredictable. (Jacques Monod, *Chance and Necessity* [New York: Knopf, 1971], p. 44)

If the study of science teaches one anything, it is that it is unwise to try to lay down beforehand by pure thought what will actually prove to be the case. Reality is often so much more subtle than we imagine. (John Polkinghorne, *The Way the World Is* [Grand Rapids: Eerdmans, 1983], p. 26)

"**W**hat sort of world do we live in?" The answer we get to this question depends on whom we ask it. If we put the question to Jacques Monod, the French Nobel Prize–winning biochemist, we are told that everything that exists is the product of chance and necessity. The universe need not have existed. Reality is like a gigantic game of roulette. The right number happened to come up, and the universe came into being. But having come into being, its existence is highly structured. Animals are machines. Human beings are machines. And humankind must come to terms with it.

If we put the same question to Albert Einstein, we get a different answer. The great discoverer of relativity laughingly dismissed the idea of a dice-playing God. "I believe," he declared, "in Spinoza's God who reveals himself in the orderly harmony of what exists, not in a God who concerns himself with the fates and actions of human beings" (P. A. Schilpp, ed., *Albert Einstein: Philosopher-Scientist* [Evanston: Library of Living Philosophers, 1949], pp. 659-60).

A GOD OF THE GAPS?

The Appeal of the God-of-the-Gaps View. The views of Jacques Monod and Albert Einstein carry weight with those who have been educated in the Western intellectual, scientific tradition. But they cut little ice with a vast number of people who cling to a God-of-the-gaps view of reality. To this group of people belong some devout churchgoers. But this group also includes many others. It counts among its ranks believers in the occult. It embraces devotees of astrology who avidly turn to the predictions of those who purport to read the stars. To its numbers also belong those faith healers who ascribe illness not to physical causes but entirely to actions of demonic powers.

According to the God-of-the-gaps view, some events in the world have natural causes and explanations. But other events do not. These are attributed to direct, supernatural intervention (whether it be God's, an angel's, a demon's, or whatever). For such people some actions are natural and some are supernatural. The supernatural is to be encountered in the gaps between the natural.

Difficulties with the God of the Gaps. The first big difficulty with a God-of-the-gaps view of reality comes when we discover a natural explanation for something that we previously thought was supernatural. The story is told of a conversation between the great French scientist Pierre-Simon de Laplace and Napoleon Bonaparte. One of Laplace's major contributions to science was his work in developing Newton's theory of the solar system. Sir Isaac Newton had never been completely convinced of the stability of the solar system. He believed that from time to time it stood in need of divine correction. God had to step into the gap left by nature. Laplace was able to provide a natural explanation for the apparent irregularities, thus prompting Napoleon to remark that he had heard that Laplace had eliminated God from his astronomy. To this Laplace replied, "Sire, I have no need of that hypothesis."

If we base our belief in God on a God-of-the-gaps view of reality, we run the risk of seeing our God shrink away like a snowman on a warm day. Each time someone comes with an explanation, a little bit of God disappears until we are left with nothing.

This brings us to the second big difficulty with the God-of-the-gaps view. It sees God only in the strange, the bizarre, the unusual. It hankers for a God of power. It fails to find God in the natural. In doing this, it effectively banishes God from the normal and the everyday. It breeds a class of believers who long for the spectacular. They want to turn ordinary events like finding a parking place for their car into an act of divine revelation. For when they run out of spectacular events to attribute to God's direct intervention, they represent to themselves the ordinary things of life as special acts of the deity, performed for their benefit.

How does all this affect miracles? The answer is clear. If an event that we thought was a miracle turns out to have a natural explanation, the God-of-the-gaps explanation turns out to be redundant and silly. If either Jacques Monod or Albert Einstein is right, belief in miracles will have to go. For Monod eliminates God from his picture of the world, while Einstein retains God but denies that God plays any active part in human affairs.

NATURAL EXPLANATIONS

The Changing Mood. To accept the views of Einstein or Monod does not mean to say that all events we call miracles never happened. On their view some of them may not have happened, and may be the product of myth, legend, pious imagination, or downright deception. Other miracle stories may, however, refer to actual events. But these must be put down to freaks or unusual coincidences for which there is no explanation at hand. Science may not have ruled out the possibility of the event. The most that could be said, on this view, is that science does not yet have an explanation for it.

To the secularized modern mind this is an attractive option. For it is less dogmatic than the answers given by the Age of Enlightenment in the eighteenth century and the skeptics of the nineteenth century. Such thinkers simply denied that miracles could have happened at all because they violated the laws of science. The modern scientist is more ready to concede that his explanations are at best incomplete. As such they are open to revision. Consequently the scientist thinks twice before dogmatizing on the basis of them. Even so, we need to realize what is being conceded. The possibility of an event happening is granted but at the expense of denying its supernatural character.

It is sometimes imagined that modern physics is more amenable to the thought of divine intervention than the classical, mechanical world of Sir Isaac Newton. But a note of caution needs to be sounded here. Modern physics has not completely overthrown Newtonian physics. Rather, it has amplified and supplemented the former views. Quantum physics does not make miracles any more feasible than they were before. The history of the debates between science and religion contain many salutary warnings against assuming that the last word has been said on any subject and against taking ideas that are valid in one field and applying them in areas that lie outside the range of their original application.

Science and Philosophy. Some views would clearly undermine a Christian outlook on God and the world. To Jacques Monod man is alone, and he knows that he is alone. Human beings are alone in a vast, unfeeling universe out of which they have emerged by chance. Neither their duty nor their destiny has been predetermined. It is up to them to make the best of it. But when we look at Monod's book, it is apparent that it is more than a scientific study. It is a philosophical proclamation that appeals to certain scientific data in order to justify a militant atheism.

The same scientific data, however, can be interpreted philosophically in different ways. On reviewing the data underlying Monod's conclusion, John Polkinghorne, who until 1979 was Professor of Mathematical Physics in the University of Cambridge, makes the comment:

> For me the beauty that it revealed was like a rehabilitation of the argument from design—not as a knockdown argument for the existence of God (there are no such arguments; nor are there for his non-existence) but as an insight into the way the world is. It is clear that the different reactions of Monod and someone like myself to the same set of scientific facts must arise from something outside the strictly scientific world view itself. (*The Way the World Is*, p. 12)

Today more than ever the real issues in the debates on science and religion do not turn on this or that particular fact. Rather, the philosophical implications (supposed or real) constitute the problem. We have just seen an instance of this in the differences between Monod and Polkinghorne. Two things need to be remembered above all.

WHAT DO WE MEAN BY "GOD"?

God's Identity. The first thing to be remembered is what we mean by "God." We need to remind ourselves that God is not a term of scientific explanation. God is not one factor alongside other factors. God cannot be tested in the same way that a factor in science can be tested. We cannot say, "God is invisible. An atom is invisible. Let's see if we can devise some experiment that will isolate and identify the activity of either of them."

The reason why we cannot do this is simple. God is not a physical entity in the same way that an atom is a physical entity. Both are invisible, but they are invisible in different ways! If they were comparable, God would actually be some kind of creature alongside other creatures.

Christian theology has always taught that God is not part of the creation (see Genesis 1 and 2; Job 38–41; Psalm 104; John 1:1-4; Acts 14:15-17; 17:27-29; Romans 1:20; 11:36; Colossians 1:16-17). He is not one entity alongside other entities. According to the biblical revelation, God is. He exists in a different way from his creatures and on his own unique plane of being. He is not dependent on them, but they are dependent on him. God is the Creator and Sustainer. He is the personal ground on which all other beings depend.

But this means that when God acts, he does not act apart from his creation but *through* it. In this life we do not see God face to face. This is something reserved in the future for the pure in heart (Matthew 5:8). Moses was told that no one shall see God's face and live (Exodus 33:20). Paul reminded Timothy that God alone has immortality "and dwells in unapproachable light, whom no man has ever seen or can see" (1 Timothy 6:16). When God acts, he acts through his creatures. The Psalmist declared that the LORD makes the winds his messengers and fire and flame his ministers (Psalm 104:4; cf. Hebrews 1:7). Paul reminded the early Christians at Rome that God is revealed through his creation. "Ever since the creation of the world his invisible nature, namely, his eternal power and deity, has been clearly perceived in the things that have been made" (Romans 1:20).

When we look at the accounts of miracles in Scripture, we never see God directly face to face. The parting of the Red Sea at the exodus was caused by God's driving the sea back by a strong east wind all night (Exodus 14:21). Then in the miracles of Jesus what we see is a before and an after. A lame man is brought to Jesus. Jesus speaks to him. The man walks. What is true here is true of the other miracles. The outward effects are depicted, but the divine cause remains hidden. Moreover, it operates through the agency of creaturely existence. Even in the supreme miracle of the incarnation, God acts through the humanity of Jesus. God did not choose to redeem us by divine fiat or some act of pure omnipotence. He chose rather the humanity of Jesus Christ, his Son, as the means by which he reconciled the world to himself.

What all this suggests is that there is a convergence of science and theology. Science claims that there are no gaps in the physical universe and that everything is in principle open to scientific explanation. Theology teaches that we should not look for divine activity in the gaps. If we are looking for God in some kind of gap, it suggests that we are looking in the wrong place or for the wrong kind of God.

Creation in Its Own Right. But biblical theology wants to make a further point, namely, that God's creation must be appreciated for what it is in its own right. The creation accounts of the Book of Genesis and the other passages of Scripture that we noted above dealing with the subject of creation speak of the orderliness and purpose of the created world. Creatures have an integrity in their own right that is not to be violated. In other words, when God has appointed something to be achieved by natural means, he is not in the habit of setting those means aside by miraculous intervention. Miracles in Scripture occur only when God has some special end that he wishes to achieve through them.

The apostle Paul bluntly reminded the Thessalonian church, "If any one will not work, let him not eat" (2 Thessalonians 3:10). Faith is no substitute for work, and work is no substitute for faith. In the parable of the good Samaritan (Luke 10) recovery comes about through loving care and attention. God has appointed healing to occur through the appropriate care, attention, and medical means. Divine healing is not an alternative fast track to this. And the use of medical means is not an alternative to turning to God in faith and prayer. In the divine structuredness of our existence God's grace is not an alternative to our human action. At the center of Christian existence stands the paradox. We are to work out our salvation with fear and trembling, living as creatures our creaturely existence in the world. But at the same time we are to realize that God is at work in us, willing and working for his good pleasure (Philippians 2:13).

But why should we believe all this? Why should we opt for the apostle Paul and the writers of the Old Testament and not go along with Einstein's Spinozism or Monod's scientific materialism? Sometime back when I was talking about the debates between science and religion, I said that two things should be remembered. I now turn to the second thing to be remembered, which has to do with the way we test ideas and theories.

TESTING CLAIMS

When we test an idea, an explanation, or a theory, two things have to be borne in mind. This applies whether we are talking about scientific ideas, historical explanations, economics, or whatever. The first thing we need to ask is, "Does the theory fit the facts of the case?" If it does not, we need to junk the theory and look for another. But then we need to go on to ask a second type of question, "How does our theory fit in with other theories?" "How does it fit our knowledge and understanding of the world at large?" If our theories and explanations do not give satisfactory answers to *both* these sets of questions, something must be wrong somewhere.

Perhaps an example may help explain the point. Most of my life is spent in a small geographical area, bounded by my home, my church, my office, and the lecture rooms where I teach. How do I know on the basis of my daily experience whether the world is round or flat? For all daily practical purposes, in going from one place to another, I could well

imagine that the world is basically flat. Nothing in my immediate experience contradicts it, although it is conceivable
that the world could be a gigantic ball so big that the curva-
ture of its surface is not normally perceptible. How do I decide whether the flat-earth theory or the round-earth theory
is correct? I opt for the latter, not because of particular observations that I personally have made, but because the round-
earth theory is compatible with my experience and is war-
ranted by the wider body of knowledge and views that I have
come to accept.

In the previous chapter we noticed C. S. Lewis arguing
along similar lines. What he was trying to do was to show
the inadequacies of materialistic determinism and to argue
the validity of a theistic view of reality. Scientific materialism
might adequately explain some things. But it could not adequately account for the human mind and our moral experience. A larger view was needed. Lewis found that view in the
Christian view of the transcendent Creator.

Broadly speaking, I think Lewis was on the right track.
But I also think it is a mistake to try to show the truth of
God and the world by arguing in the abstract. The attempt
to prove the existence of God first and then to show that this
God is the God of Christian faith is full of pitfalls. Suppose,
for the purposes of argument, that the rational structures we
find in nature are best explained by presupposing a "cosmic
mind." How then do we get from a "cosmic mind" to the
God with all the various qualities attributed to him in the
Bible? How do we show that the "cosmic mind" is the same
as the God of the Bible? How do we get from a "cosmic mind"
to a Trinity? We can get from the one to the other only by a
leap of faith or by deliberately ignoring the differences.

But the biblical writers never argued from an abstract
God of natural theology to the living God of their faith. Rather,
they presented their faith as the true explanation of their experience and their perception of the world. They did not move
from reason to faith. Rather, it was from the standpoint of

their faith that they were able to express both the mystery and the rationality of life. In other words, their apprehension of God as the Creator and Redeemer not only made sense of their experience of the world but gave them strength to live by.

WHERE DO MIRACLES FIT IN?

I have personally never met anyone who came to faith because he or she was persuaded by philosophical arguments about the existence of God. But I know of many people who came to faith in God in some way or other and who then found that philosophical arguments helped to clarify their thinking. Very few people today seem to come to faith because of miracles. Most often it seems that people find that God in Christ meets their deepest needs. And then perhaps to their surprise and disquiet they find that *this* God is reputed in Scripture to have worked miracles.

He does not seem to be working them all the time. For great stretches of history in the Old Testament and in the Christian church there seem to be no miracles at all. But in the Bible Jesus is certainly said to have wrought miracles. How are we to think of miracles? We shall try to answer this question in the next chapter. But before we do so, we may remind ourselves of some perceptive comments made half a century ago by the Cambridge professor H. H. Farmer. In looking at miracles and the laws of nature, Farmer observed:

> The question . . . is not one of causation as against non-causation, or of order against disorder, but whether a certain type of causation and order, namely that involved in the idea of God initiating events in accordance with His wisdom in relation to individual situations, is so contradictory of that type of causation and order which science presupposes and investigates that we are forced to choose between them, and believe either in miracles or in science, but not in both. (*The World and God* [London: Nisbet, 2nd ed. 1936], pp. 145-46)

To Farmer it was rather like looking at a piece of embroidery. If you look at one side, you see a beautiful, intricate pattern. If you turn it over and look at the other side, you might see a lot of crisscrossing threads and knots. Science is like looking at the crisscrossing threads. It explains how things behave. But it does not answer the metaphysical and theological questions of why they behave as they do.

Farmer saw an analogy between our relationship to the world and God's relationship to the world. As personal beings we are related to a system that can be described in terms of causes and effects. When I turn on the light, or switch on the ignition in my car, or eat something, or do anything at all, I am not violating any law of nature. I am not suspending any sequence of cause and effect. Rather, I am initiating some sequences and terminating others. I live in the world, but as a personal being I transcend it.

How do we think of actions of God? It is unrealistic to think of God operating in the gaps and acting only outside his created order. According to the biblical writers, God does not suspend nature. He acts on it and with it.

6 / What Then Is a Miracle?

I call that a miracle, whatever appears that is difficult or unusual above the hope or power of them who wonder. (Augustine, *On the Profit of Believing*, §34)

"What then is a miracle?" The question can be answered on two levels—the philosophical and the theological.

A QUESTION ON TWO LEVELS

If we ask the question on the philosophical level, we are asking a formal and a logical question. We are asking questions like "What distinguishes a miracle from an ordinary event?" "How do we recognize miracles?" "What kind of justification would we need before we could say that this event was a miracle?" These are philosophical questions. For philosophy has to do with the logic or argument, the scrutiny of truth claims, and the analysis of the meaning of statements.

But when we ask "What is a miracle?" on a theological level, we are asking a rather different set of questions. Theology is the account that we give of God and of his relations with the world. And Christian theology is the attempt to say what we know about God in the light of his revelation of himself in Jesus Christ. This in turn means asking "What do we know about God from the Scriptures?" So when we ask "What is a miracle?" on the level of Christian theology, we are asking questions like "What can we gather about miracles from our reading of the Bible?" "What is the place and purpose of miracles in God's scheme of things?" "What is the point of miracle stories?"

We need to ask the question "What is a miracle?" on both these levels. I shall begin with the philosophical level. But before I do so, I must give a word of warning. The warning is simply that the same thinker can wear more than one hat. When we read the writings of wide-ranging thinkers like Saint Augustine or C. S. Lewis, we need to remember that sometimes they are doing philosophy and sometimes they are doing theology. And sometimes philosophy encroaches upon theology and theology encroaches upon philosophy. So we should not be unduly surprised if, when we look at the philosophical question, we find ourselves sometimes listening to what the theologians have to say.

THE PHILOSOPHICAL QUESTION

Let's begin then with the philosophical question. In Chapter 4 we saw C. S. Lewis's answer to the question "What is a miracle?" Lewis replied that when he used the word "miracle," he meant "an interference with Nature by supernatural power." I think Lewis was on the right track. For the reasons I spelled out in the last two chapters I think we get on the wrong track if we try to locate all God's activity in the gaps in nature. Lewis rightly stressed the role of divine initiative, and sought to give nature her due place. Belief in miracles does not require us to suspend all belief in natural and secondary causes. Rather, it calls for our willingness to envisage the possibility of God's ordering of nature to achieve his purposes, and of bringing into play factors outside the realm of scientific understanding.

Are All Divine Interferences Miracles? In a broad sense, yes. For the word "miracle" suggests a wonder without necessarily implying that any law of nature has been violated or superseded. It comes from the Latin *miraculum*, which means a wonder, a prodigy, a miracle. It is linked with the verb *mirari*, "to wonder," "to be astonished at." A miracle in this sense causes wonder and astonishment.

In line with this is the open-ended definition of Augustine at the beginning of this chapter. We looked at Augustine in Chapter 1, but it is worthwhile to retrace our steps at this point in the discussion, for Augustine saw the issues as clearly as anyone. He distinguished two types of miracles. Some miracles only provoke wonder. But others bring real benefits to people. If people were to see a man flying across the sky, it would only cause them to wonder. But the healing work of Jesus did more than cause wonder. It brought relief and wholeness to broken and hurting bodies. It was like a hidden sign of the healing that Christ brought to the soul. *The miracles of Jesus pointed men and women to God.*

Why Not More Miracles? But if miracles were as good as all that, why did God not do more of them? Augustine's reply is a good one. He pointed out how easily people can get into the habit of not being moved unless they see a wonder. They want something bigger and better each time. They cease to wonder at the usual. If familiarity does not exactly breed contempt, it often breeds indifference. People are always wanting something new and different. There is a kind of spirituality that just lives for the spiritual highs. The marvels of nature and the wonders of God's daily goodness are so ordinary that people take them for granted.

Nevertheless, nature brings before us a continuous procession of miracles. The changing of the seasons, the beauty of light, the phenomenon of growth from tiny seeds, and the endless variety of sounds, tastes, and colors that surround us—all these are truly wonderful, and Christian faith traces them to God's activity in creation and providence. If we encountered any of these phenomena only once, we would say that it was a miracle. But they happen over and over again all the time. The result is that we just take them for granted. If

God were to do more often the special things that we call miracles, we would take them for granted in just the same way. Augustine concluded that God deliberately chose to do them only when they fulfilled some special purpose. We are to love God not for the sake of miracles but for his own sake.

Two Types of Miracles. Augustine believed that miracles were not necessarily contrary to nature, but only to what we *know* of nature. In saying this Augustine anticipated what a number of modern thinkers are saying about miracles. A case in point is philosopher R. F. Holland's celebrated discussion "The Miraculous" (*American Philosophical Quarterly* II [1965]: 43-51).

Holland draws a distinction between the *contingency* or *coincidence concept* of the miraculous and the *violation concept*. As a case of the former, Holland tells the story of a child riding a toy car onto a railroad crossing. The car gets stuck, and the child does not see the oncoming train or heed the mother's efforts to warn him of danger. But the train stops and a terrible accident is averted. The reason, however, was not that the driver saw the child in time. The driver had been taken ill. He released pressure on the control lever and the brakes came on automatically. In this case no laws of nature were violated. All the factors in the situation are normal occurrences. What is unique in the situation is the coincidence of them.

Turning to the *violation concept* of miracle, Holland lays down two conditions that would have to be fulfilled before any event of this type could be regarded as a miracle. On the one hand, it must be impossible in the light of our understanding of nature. For if it were not impossible, then it would be just another ordinary event. On the other hand, it must have happened. Otherwise it would be a nonevent.

Holland's approach certainly has its attractions. It has provoked a lot of discussion. But does it really work? Are there any clear-cut examples of the *violation* type of miracle of which we could say that they were impossible, but never-

theless that they had certainly happened? Holland's own examples are not entirely free from objections of one kind or
another. Two of them are purely hypothetical: a horse kept
alive without food, and levitation without physical support.
These examples certainly meet the first of Holland's two
tests. They are clearly violations of the laws of nature. But
they fail the second of his tests—that the event in question
actually happened—precisely because they are given as *hypothetical* examples.

Holland's other example of an instance of the *violation
concept* of miracle is also not free from difficulties. It is the
story of water turned into wine at Cana (John 2). Here again
the difficulty lies in the fact that the historicity of the story
has not been established by corroborative evidence. To grasp
this point we need to realize that there is an important distinction between believing something and being able to prove
that that something happened. When we look at the story of
the wedding feast at Cana, it is clear that we have only John's
word for it. It is not mentioned in the other three Gospels or
anywhere else in the New Testament for that matter.

This is not to say that the events described in John 2
never happened. But it is to recognize that we do not have
the multiple attestation that historians see as vital in establishing the veracity of reports—especially of reports concerning the unusual and alleged events that run contrary to
experience.

If we say that we believe the event happened because
it is described in John's Gospel and because John's Gospel is
part of divinely inspired Scripture, we need to remind ourselves precisely what we are doing. We have, in fact, stood on
its head the traditional argument concerning miracles. The
traditional argument went like this: we believe the teaching
contained in the account because it is authorized by the miracle. Now we are saying: we believe the miracle because it
is attested in the account that is authorized by the divine
inspiration of Scripture. The argument is logical, but it is a

complete reversal of the traditional argument. It makes the historicity of the event in question depend not on historical corroboration of the account, but on the prior belief-commitments of the reader. The upshot is that we cannot claim that the event in question has really met the second of Holland's two tests.

When we turn back to the *contingency* or *coincidence concept* of miracle, we are confronted with the opposite problem. The problem is not to show that the event in question actually happened. The problem now is to show that the event was not just a matter of coincidence or luck. In the case of the little boy and his toy car all the elements in the situation are credible in and of themselves. Why then should we say that it is a miracle and not a stroke of luck?

We all know of similar situations. Just recently a lady told me how her granddaughter had been miraculously missed by a truck that plowed into a storefront. It was only by "accident" that the child's father looked up and saw the truck heading straight for them and out of control. He managed to snatch the little girl away just in time.

And what about cases of healing? Sometimes we pray for someone, knowing full well that the chances of recovery are good. Sometimes the chances are less than good. When are we entitled to call a recovery a miracle? Must there be a complete absence of medical care before we can do this? Can we prove that the recovery would not have happened if we had not prayed for it?

What Is Involved in Believing and Rejecting? The more I look at these questions the more I am brought back to the importance of analogy and of what I have earlier called our frame of reference (see Chapter 3). Take the question "Should I accept an event for which there is only one item of evidence?" The event need not have anything to do with the miraculous. It may be, say, a story about Julius Caesar or George Washington. Does the historian reject the story because it was told by only one person? No. The historian has to ask further questions. If the source reporting the story is known to be generally reliable, the historian is inclined to accept testimony from that source. If the reported story fits in with what we know of Julius Caesar or George Washington, and if the event in question is feasible, then the historian may be inclined to accept it as a historical event. It is not inherently infeasible to think of Julius Caesar riding a horse in Gaul or of George Washington riding in a carriage in Virginia. But it is downright absurd to think of either of them traveling by car or plane.

The decisive factor here is not the sincerity of the report but the background convictions that we bring to the report and that constitute our frame of reference for evaluating the report. A great deal of what we accept as historical depends on relatively slight evidence—evidence that is not independently corroborated by another source. The decision to accept or reject depends on the strength of the inclining factors in the situation, which in turn determine our frame of reference.

In Chapter 3 we looked at the curious case of the King of Siam. The King refused to believe in ice because he had no experience of water ever solidifying and because he could not conceive of any circumstances under which it could. If the King had not been trapped by his limited experience, he would have been more open to receive news of something that transcended his understanding.

The story of the King of Siam brings into focus the basic issue. The decisive factor in judging whether to believe or not to believe a report is not necessarily the report itself. It is our background understanding of what is feasible and what is not. This background understanding or frame of reference (or whatever we prefer to call it) works in two ways. As we have just seen, it helps us to decide whether we think a reported event happened or not. And it also affects how we interpret events.

In Chapter 4 we saw how C. S. Lewis was concerned to set the whole question of miracles within the frame of reference of a worldview. Only against the background of a personal Creator who could interfere with the nature that he had created did miracle stories make sense. Without this background miracle stories make no sense. On the other hand, they become still more feasible if we see them in the context of the "grand miracle" of the incarnation, in which God himself is personally present in a human life. From the standpoint of our common experience of death, the New Testament accounts of Jesus' resurrection may appear incredible. But in the context of a vision of a new created order of which the risen Christ is the firstfruits, the New Testament teaching about the resurrection takes on a new meaning and a new credibility.

Are we then to conclude that it is all a matter of preconceived ideas? Are we saying that some people believe in miracles because they have made up their minds to believe in advance, while others disbelieve because they too have made up their minds beforehand?

I do not think that we can get out of this dilemma simply by following C. S. Lewis. Lewis tried to establish the feasibility of the New Testament miracle stories by first trying to show that belief in a personal "cosmic mind" made more sense of our human experience in the world than materialistic atheism. But it is one thing to believe in a personal "cosmic mind"; it is something else to believe in the miracle-working God of the New Testament. C. S. Lewis did not show how he got from one to the other. He could only do it by assuming that the two Gods were the same. In other words, he got from one to the other either by an assumption or by a leap of faith.

A Line of Approach. The approach that I want to suggest is slightly different. Belief in God is never a matter of clear-cut proof or knockdown argument. As the writer of the Epistle to the Hebrews suggests (Hebrews 11:3), the Christian view of creation is as much a faith doctrine as any other doctrine. At bottom it involves a perception of God that is given to us. But it is not just a blind belief. It is a perception of God that enables us to make sense of the world we live in. In fact, it makes better sense of the world and of our experience than such rival alternatives as materialistic atheism, pantheism, sheer agnosticism, and the rest.

In other words, instead of trying to get to God in two stages (as C. S. Lewis does by arguing abstractly for a "cosmic mind" and then jumping to the God of the Bible), it is better to start with the God of the Bible as the one who meets our needs and answers our questions. We must frankly acknowledge that this is a faith position. But then all positions are ultimately faith positions of one sort or another—even atheism and materialism. For they all involve commitments that are then justified or falsified by their ability to explain the situation. Christians believe that the personal Creator-Redeemer God of the Bible makes more sense of the human cosmic situation than his rivals. Moreover, they testify to the transforming love of *this* God in their lives.

The God who declares himself to be the Creator and our heavenly Father is also declared to be a God who continues to be active in his creation. He is even said to interfere with the normal order of things in special circumstances for the good of his children. In other words, Christianity presents us with a package of beliefs. These beliefs are interrelated, and we cannot simply pick and choose what we want to accept out of the total package.

From biblical times onward some men and women have come to faith because of miracles. But for many people today miracles are a secondary issue. They may have turned to Christ because of their need to be delivered from their sins. They may have turned to him because of their own deep-felt inadequacy. It may have been only after they had found their needs met that they discovered that the Christ who met their needs is also said in the Gospels to have been a miracle-working Christ. In this case the miracle stories are not the foundation of faith. They are part of the total picture of God in Christ. Their feasibility depends not on the strength of testimony to any given story, but on their feasibility in the context of the total picture of God in Christ.

We shall have more to say on this score in the next few chapters. We have still to look at the question "What is a miracle?" from the more strictly theological standpoint. But before we do so we need to comment on two further points raised by the *contingency* or *coincidence concept* of miracle.

The first of these points can be put in the form of a question. *"How do we know that this is a real miracle and not just luck or fortuitous circumstances?"* Someone who believes in luck will say that the story of the child's being saved from the train was just another lucky break. Someone who does not believe in much of anything might well say that it was all just a matter of circumstances. But a religious person might say that it was another sign of God's providential care. What these people are doing is interpreting the same event in terms of their respective frames of reference.

How can we break the deadlock? How can we tell which one is right? The answer to these questions depends on two factors. The first of these factors is the answer to the question "How good is my frame of reference?" Is belief in luck or circumstances really adequate to explain the situation and also really adequate as an account of life in general? Belief in luck or fortuitous circumstances may explain this or that, but in the long run it fails as a total explanation of life. But a religious person is able to relate the particular experience to a wider view of God's working as a whole. The second of these factors that helps us decide between the rival views is simply the experience people have of God touching their lives. Sometimes we sense a guiding presence in the events that make up our experience. When our experience coincides with the framework of our beliefs, we get both a sharper perception of our experience and a confirmation of our beliefs.

The second of our points concerning the *contingency concept* of miracle may also be put in the form of a question. *"Is it conceivable that all miracles might ultimately turn out to be instances of contingency or coincidence?"* From our present human standpoint it looks as if the answer to this question must be no. Clearly some miracles in the Bible admit the presence of natural factors. The plagues in Egypt (Exodus 8–10) contain a series of natural disasters. The parting of the Red Sea was caused by "a strong east wind" blowing all night (Exodus 14:21). The providential provision of manna and quails likewise has a natural side to it. Some of the healing stories may have involved psychosomatic factors. But other miracle stories contain no such factors. Clearly, an event like the resurrection of Jesus involves more than a series of naturally explicable circumstances.

But if Christian thinkers like Augustine and C. S. Lewis are right, miracles are not simply random events. God is not a God of chaos. Miracles are not necessarily unrepeatable events that science cannot explain. The reason why science cannot explain them is not that they do not belong to any order at all, but that they do not belong to the *natural* order. If we look carefully at passages like 1 Corinthians 15 and 1 John 3:2, we find that Paul and John did not think of Jesus' resurrection as an absolutely unique event. It was, as it were, the prototype of the resurrection of believers generally. It represents the incursion of the new order into our present order. Such events defy our human understanding. They do not belong to our present range of experience. From our standpoint they clearly violate what we *know* of nature. But from God's standpoint, according to the New Testament, they have their place as part of God's new creation.

Summary. To sum up, I would say that we begin at the wrong end if we start by thinking of miracles basically as violations of the laws of nature. Miracles are not random occurrences but expressions of God's purposeful, gracious activity. In some cases they may violate what we know of nature. But in other cases there may be no violation at all. The important point is God's providential ordering of events. If we think of a miracle as God's interference with nature, we have to remember that God may interfere in various ways. One way of interfering would be for God to initiate something and then let nature take its normal course. An example of this would be a case of miraculous healing in which the course of an illness was arrested by divine intervention followed by the recovery of the body in a normal way.

In cases where an alleged miracle appears to violate the natural order we are still not dealing with a random event from a Christian point of view. From the standpoint of our understanding of nature it violates our scientific understanding of the world, which is founded on generalizations based on observed, repeated experience. Whereas miracles may be repeated, they have not been repeated in such numbers as to enable scientists to formulate "laws" concerning them. On the other hand, from the standpoint of faith such miracles appear to have their own "laws." They represent not the abandonment of all order but the breaking into our present world order of the order of the world to come. The resurrection of Jesus is the prime example of this type of miracle. It presents the greatest instance of God's interfering with nature by introducing the order of the new creation into our present order.

Neither science nor philosophy can disprove the possibility of miracles. The most they can do is to declare their improbability, when viewed within the frame of reference supplied by our normal experience. But from this standpoint no one has ever imagined that miracles were anything other than improbable. The question of whether they are feasible is another matter. We cannot understand miracles. But we can grasp something of their possibility and purpose when we approach them within the context of a worldview that sees God as the sovereign, personal Creator and Sustainer of the universe. The question whether such a personal God has ever miraculously intervened in the normal order of the world can be decided only by examining the evidence in the light of our fundamental convictions about the nature of God and reality. It is to this question that we must turn in Part II of this book. But before we do so it is worth looking at how the biblical writers answer the question "What then is a miracle?"

THE THEOLOGICAL QUESTION

Miracles in the Old Testament. The Old Testament speaks of "signs and wonders." The basic respective Hebrew terms here are *ôt* (sign, pledge, token) and *môpēt* (wonder, sign, portent). The two words occur together in the warning of Deuteronomy 13:1-3 that became decisive for Jewish attitudes to miracles: "If a prophet arises among you, or a dreamer of dreams, and gives you a sign or a wonder, and the sign or wonder he tells you comes to pass, and if he says, 'Let us go after other gods,' which you have not known, 'and let us serve them,' you shall not listen to the words of that prophet or to that dreamer of dreams; for the LORD your God is testing you, to know whether you love the LORD your God with all your heart and with all your soul."

Not only is the worker of such signs and wonders to be disregarded. He is to be put to death so that the evil may be purged out of the midst of the people of God (Deuteronomy 13:5-11).

But signs and wonders are not necessarily the work of false prophets. Yahweh himself performed signs and wonders in bringing his people out of Egypt (Exodus 7:3; Deuteronomy 4:34; 6:22; 7:19; 26:8; 29:3; Nehemiah 9:10; Psalms 78:43; 105:27; 135:9; Jeremiah 32:20-21). The decisive thing here is the relationship of the sign to Yahweh. This is recognized in the light of the teaching that accompanies it, the previous acts of Yahweh, and continuing knowledge of him. In other words, if we may use the language used in the philosophical part of our discussion, signs and wonders have a frame of reference that enables the onlooker and the hearer to determine whether they are of God or not.

In the Old Testament signs are not necessarily violations of what we know of nature. The sun and the moon are signs (Genesis 1:14). So too is circumcision (Genesis 17:11). But it is a characteristic of signs to point beyond themselves to Yahweh's ordering or overriding of nature and history. The blood of the Passover lamb was a sign (Exodus 12:13), as was the sign of Immanuel (Isaiah 7:11, 14) and Ahaz's sundial (Isaiah 38:7). Signs confirmed that Yahweh would do what he had undertaken (Exodus 4:1-10), or embodied and exemplified his saving action (Exodus 7:1-17).

A wonder could carry with it the suggestion of a threat or warning (Exodus 11:9; Deuteronomy 28:46). It indicated Yahweh's control of nature (Psalms 71:7; 105:5; Isaiah 8:18; 20:3; Zechariah 3:8). The Old Testament also speaks of wonders, marvels (Exodus 15:11; Psalms 77:12, 14; 78:12; 88:10, 12; 89:5; Isaiah 25:1), and God's wonderful deeds (Exodus 3:20; Judges 6:13; Psalms 9:1; 26:7). Meditation on Yahweh's great and terrible acts is cause for praise and encouragement (2 Samuel 7:23; 1 Chronicles 17:19; Psalms 105:5; 145:5-6).

When we look back at the Old Testament one fact stands out in stark relief. Signs and wonders were not everyday occurrences. They were very rare. Only occasionally is supernatural healing mentioned, as in the Elijah and Elisha stories (1 Kings 17; 2 Kings 4–5). And even in these stories it is not frequent. Often signs and wonders involve judgments on the enemies of the people of God. Above all, signs and wonders occur at critical points in the history of God's saving dealings with his people.

Miracles in the New Testament. When we turn to the New Testament we again keep coming across the expression "signs and wonders" (*sēmeia kai terata* in the Greek). The expression occurs in Matthew 24:24 and Mark 13:22 (which repeat the warning of Deuteronomy 13); Acts 2:19 (which quotes Joel 2:30); Acts 2:22, 43; 4:30; 5:12; 6:8; 7:36; 15:12; Romans 15:19; 2 Corinthians 12:12; 2 Thessalonians 2:9; Hebrews 2:4. Signs and wonders are wrought by God as a testimony. But they may also be performed by false prophets who seek to deceive. The disciples asked Jesus for a sign of his coming and the close of the age (Matthew 24:3; Mark 13:4; cf. Luke 21:11, 25-26). Jesus warned them against being deceived, and spoke of the coming violent times.

Both Jesus and Paul deprecated the desire for signs (Matthew 12:39; 16:4; cf. Luke 11:16, 19; John 4:48; 1 Corinthians 1:22). The demand for a sign is indicative of a refusal to respond to what has already been given.

The word "sign" (*sēmeion*) is found on its own in addition to its use in the phrase "signs and wonders." It comes in the request to Jesus for a sign and his saying about the sign of Jonah (Matthew 12:38-39; Luke 11:29-30; cf. Matthew 16:1, 3-4; Mark 8:11-12; Luke 11:16). It occurs in the sayings about the sign of the parousia (Matthew 24:3; Mark 13:4; Luke 21:7; cf. Matthew 24:30; Luke 21:11, 25), and the signs mentioned in the longer ending of Mark's Gospel (Mark 16:17, 20). Luke also mentions signs in his birth narratives, and observes that Herod hoped to see Jesus perform a sign (Luke 23:8).

The word "sign" is characteristic of the Fourth Gospel, where it is used to denote Jesus' miracles (John 2:11, 18, 23; 3:2; 4:54; 6:2; 7:31; 9:16; 10:41; 11:47; 12:18, 37; 20:30). The signs of Jesus are grounds for faith. At the same time John describes Jesus' miracles as works. The works of Jesus are also the works of the Father (John 4:34; 5:20, 36; 7:3, 21; 9:3-4; 10:25, 32-33, 37-38; 14:10-12; 15:24; 17:4; cf. Matthew 11:2, 19; Luke 24:19). The verb "to work" is also used to describe God's or Jesus' work (John 3:21; 5:17; 6:27-28, 30; 9:4). Jesus frequently did his works of healing on the sabbath, and the choice of the term "work" to describe his healings serves to underline the differences between Jesus and his Jewish opponents in their understanding of what was permissible on the sabbath.

Finally, the word *dynamis,* "power," is used of a deed of power, or mighty work. Most often it occurs in the plural "mighty works" (Matthew 7:22; 11:20-21, 23; 13:54, 58; Mark 6:5; Luke 10:13; 19:37; Acts 2:22). The mighty works of Jesus are presented as grounds for response. Failure to respond is blameworthy. The mighty works wrought by Christians in the early church are attributed to the Spirit (1 Corinthians 12:10, 28-29; Galatians 3:5; Hebrews 2:4; 6:5). They belong to the signs of an apostle (2 Corinthians 12:12).

What is the meaning and significance of all this? I shall try to give my answer in Parts II and III of this book.

II / What Do the
Miracle Stories
Tell Us about Jesus?

7 / The Quest of the Unhistorical Jesus

The Christ that Harnack sees, looking back through nineteen centuries of Catholic darkness, is only the reflection of a Liberal Protestant face, seen at the bottom of a deep well. (George Tyrrell, *Christianity at the Cross-Roads* [1909], p. 44)

Ever since people began to doubt whether miracles could happen people have also wondered whether Jesus really performed them. For the past two centuries and more scholars have been engaged in what has come to be called the quest of the historical Jesus.

What was Jesus really like? To many the Christ of Christian theology—and, for that matter, the Christ of the New Testament—is like an official portrait painted by a court painter. It is the work of devout veneration, but not a true likeness. Art and pious imagination have improved on nature. What is therefore needed is to strip away the official portrait of Jesus as a wonder-working divine being in human form and get back to Jesus as he must have been—Jesus as simply a man.

In this chapter we shall sketch the course of the quest of the historical Jesus. We shall note some of the chief highlights, and we shall also ask what they mean for us today. All too often the results were disappointing. What Tyrrell said about Harnack was true of many other scholars. The Christ they saw was really a reflection of themselves or their own ideas. Nevertheless, we cannot escape the questions "What was Jesus really like?" "Is our picture of him founded on history?"

THE QUEST GETS UNDER WAY

The Fragments Controversy. Ever since Albert Schweitzer published his masterly *Quest of the Historical Jesus* in 1906 scholars have been in the habit of tracing the quest back to Hermann Samuel Reimarus. Reimarus was a scholarly teacher who lived in Hamburg. He was known for his learned, if somewhat dry, writings on the rationality of nature and religion. But he was also the author of a private work that was not intended for publication. It contained the distillation of doubts nursed over a lengthy period. Parts of the work were published after his death as *Fragments of an Unnamed Author* (1778).

The complete work ranged widely over the whole field of the Bible. But Reimarus's skepticism reached its zenith in the section purporting to deal with "The Intentions of Jesus and His Disciples." Reimarus depicted Jesus as a Jewish reformer who mixed politics with religion in a vain attempt to establish the Kingdom of God on earth. He completely miscalculated popular support, and misguidedly reckoned on God's coming to his aid.

After Jesus' death the disciples (who had not done an honest day's work for some years) thought up a scheme to maintain the good life to which they had grown accustomed. They put out the story that Jesus had been raised from the dead and that he would return one day. In fact, said Reimarus, they had stolen the body of Jesus and hidden it where no one could find it. Nevertheless, the hoax they had perpetrated took in an enormous number of people. From that day to this, people have gone on believing the story. Only a handful have realized that Christianity is built upon a gigantic fraud.

The publication of Reimarus's *Fragment* on Jesus

caused a loud theological explosion that rocked the German churches. Albert Schweitzer described it as a bolt from the blue. Reimarus, he said, "had no predecessors; neither had he any disciples." But Schweitzer was only half right.

When the dust settled after the explosion, no disciples were to be found. But Reimarus did, in fact, have a number of predecessors in the shape of the English Deists. We encountered some of them in Chapter 2. Reimarus himself was in England when the Deistic controversy was nearing its zenith. He had in his personal library a substantial collection of their writings. And the *Fragments* themselves were part of a larger defense of the Deists as "Rational Worshippers of God."

Reimarus was not starting a completely new line of thought. He was, in fact, standing in the same basic tradition of European rational skepticism as Hume and Spinoza. Although Hume and Spinoza differed on many points, they were agreed on one thing. Supernatural interventions could not be admitted into history. Nature presents us with a closed system that can be explained in terms of natural laws. Everything that might appear to conflict with the laws of nature must be discounted. Everything, therefore, must have a rational, natural explanation.

Fictitious Lives of Jesus. In the years that followed hundreds of scholars gave their own variations on this theme. Some were wild and fanciful. Others were sober and earnest.

As the eighteenth century drew to its close Carl Friedrich Bahrdt wrote a fictitious life of Jesus around a plot worthy of a first-century James Bond. Jesus was pictured as a kind of front man who was adopted by the Essenes in their attempt to take over Jewish society. Jesus had already picked up a rudimentary medical knowledge concerning infections and nervous disorders. The various other miracles were faked. The crucifixion was rigged by Nicodemus. Luke, the physician, had already given Jesus some pain-killing drugs. As soon as Jesus was taken down from the cross, Luke set about the task of resuscitation in the cave where Joseph of Arimathea had had him placed. From time to time Jesus made rare public appearances. He continued to play a key part in the Essene organization until he died of natural causes.

Similar ideas were repeated by Karl Heinrich Venturini. who likewise made abundant use of the Essenes. The Essene Order was particularly convenient to such writers because it was known to exist from the brief references to it in various ancient writings, and yet nobody at the time knew much about it. Bahrdt and Venturini felt free to attribute to the Essenes whatever they cared without fear of contradiction.

Rationalistic Lives of Jesus. Across the Atlantic in America, Thomas Jefferson's account of Jesus was a much more sober affair. He had gotten to know Deism and skepticism firsthand while visiting Europe. Although a practicing Episcopalian, Jefferson was thoroughly Deistic in his views of religion. The so-called *Jefferson Bible* was literally a scissors and paste production. Jefferson cut up four copies of the Gospels. He cut out all references to the Virgin Birth, angels, miracles, the Holy Spirit, and the resurrection of Jesus. He pasted what was left into a book that he called *The Life and Morals of Jesus of Nazareth Extracted Textually from the Gospels in Greek, Latin, French and English.* It contained the barest account of Jesus' life and teaching and was basically devoid of God and the supernatural.

In the meantime, back on the Continent a number of scholars were beginning to write rationalistic lives of Jesus. In his *Life of Jesus* (1828) H. E. G. Paulus suggested natural explanations for Jesus' healings. He explained Jesus' resuscitations of people like Jairus's daughter as the emergence from a coma that had been wrongly diagnosed. Jesus did not really walk on the water. He was actually standing on the shore. His features and position were obscured by the mist. The five thousand were really fed by those who had brought with them something to eat, and were shamed into sharing their provisions. Jesus' resurrection was not really a return from death. He had merely lost consciousness and was revived by the cool atmosphere in the tomb and by the earthquake.

K. A. von Hase's *Life of Jesus* (1829) was more restrained. Wherever possible, he looked for natural explanations provided they did not conflict too much with what the New Testament actually said. Hase believed that the healing miracles of Jesus could be explained psychosomatically. Jesus' miraculous gift appeared to Hase to be "a dominion of Spirit over nature." What had been lost to mankind through the fall and human sin "was restored in Jesus' holy innocence to its ancient bounds against the abnormal nature of disease and death."

In an attempt to make the nature miracles of Jesus more credible, Hase suggested that they may have been instances of natural processes, accelerated in accordance with laws unknown to us. The feeding of the five thousand was a case in point. "If nature annually brings about a similar wonder in the time between sowing and harvest, she could perhaps bring it about by an unknown law in a moment."

Strauss and the Question of Myth. But such explanations failed to satisfy David Friedrich Strauss. In his *Life of Jesus Critically Examined* (1835) Strauss brushed aside both orthodoxy and rationalism. The orthodox were too gullible in taking the Bible at face value, and the rationalists were looking for the wrong sort of rational explanation. All, according to Strauss, had failed to see that most of the stories about Jesus were really myths.

The miracle stories had come into being through the pious myth-making of the early Christians who saw Jesus through the rose-colored glasses of the Old Testament. Job addressed God as one who "trampled the waves of the sea" (Job 9:8). The early Christians saw Jesus doing the same thing

(Matthew 14:25; Mark 6:48; John 6:19). Anything Moses or Elijah could do Jesus could do better.

In short, Strauss's book was written to show that the Jesus of the Gospels was the product of the religious imagination of the first Christians.

Strauss entertained the possibility that Jesus had actually healed some people. In such cases psychological factors must have come into play. But for the rest Strauss rejected divine interventions in history as beyond belief in view of the modern understanding of science and nature. The idea of God becoming man in the figure of Jesus was really the symbolic religious expression of the truth of Hegelian philosophy. It was the mythological symbol of the infinite spirit in the finite spirits of all human beings.

A French Life of Jesus. Perhaps the nearest French equivalent to Strauss was J. E. Renan. But Renan's *Life of Jesus* (1863) took a different course. Renan had little to say about myth. He left standing the outline of events described in the Gospels. He simply cut out the supernatural. "Miracles are things which never happen; only credulous people believe they have seen them." "We reject the supernatural for the same reason that we reject the existence of centaurs and hippogriffes; and this reason is, that nobody has ever seen them." The Gospels were really legends. They might contain history. But not everything they contained was historical. In Renan's hands, the Christ of the Gospels became a sublime idealist striding through the Holy Land.

Renan's book was reprinted over and over in French and many other languages. It was more impressive as a historical novel than as historical research. Renan himself admitted that much of his book was guesswork. But the book's success was not due simply to its narrative verve. There was a market for a secularized version of Christianity, and Renan met it. He gave people a Christ whom they could understand but in whom they did not need to believe.

An English Life of Jesus. In England Sir John Seeley's *Ecce Homo* (1865) bore the marks of a traditional English reserve. Seeley confessed that miracles in themselves were "extremely improbable things." But he did not deny them outright. He just insisted that they could not be admitted "unless supported by a great concurrence of evidence." Seeley's account of Jesus reads like an extended obituary for a very great man. What impressed Seeley about Jesus was "the moral miracle," Jesus' "temperance in his use of supernatural power." Jesus' mission in life was to establish the Kingdom of God on earth. In theological language it meant striving that God's will may be done on earth as it is in heaven. In everyday language it meant "the improvement of morality."

Seeley's views represent a type of Victorian liberal Protestantism that had its counterparts in America and Europe. It was a version of Christianity that stressed the moral side of religion. It depicted Jesus as the greatest moral and religious teacher the world had ever seen. Jesus was a historical figure all right. But what was special about him was his keen moral insights, his personal integrity, and his sublime teaching.

Schleiermacher's Alternative. It was this portrait of Jesus that came to characterize liberal theology in the second half of the nineteenth century. Of course, the details varied from theologian to theologian. Earlier in the century Friedrich Schleiermacher at Berlin had stressed the importance of religious experience. He had even used it as a key to understanding the personality of Jesus. To Schleiermacher the essence of religion was a sense of dependence. He depicted sin as our attempt to be independent when we were meant to live our lives in conscious dependence on God. Schleiermacher saw Jesus as a man who at every moment of his life was utterly dependent on God. Jesus was so consciously dependent on God that you could even say that God existed in his life.

This was Schleiermacher's way of explaining the incarnation. It attracted a following among those who had given up on orthodoxy. Echoes of it can still be heard in liberal theology to this day. But by the end of the nineteenth century the voices that could be heard above all the rest were those of men like Ritschl and Harnack who stressed the moral side of Christianity.

In his popular lectures *What Is Christianity?* delivered at the University of Berlin (1900) Harnack summed up the teaching of Jesus under three heads: (1) the Kingdom of God and its coming; (2) God the Father and the infinite value of the human soul; and (3) the higher righteousness and the commandment of love. It was this book that prompted George Tyrrell's comment, "The Christ that Harnack sees, looking back through nineteen centuries of Catholic darkness, is only the reflection of a Liberal Protestant face, seen at the bottom of a deep well."

THE QUEST GRINDS TO A HALT

Tyrrell was not the only one who felt that something was wrong with the liberal picture of Jesus. Despite all the talk about sound historical methods and the importance of biblical criticism the portrait of Jesus that emerged looked suspiciously like that of an earnest Victorian idealist wearing first-century Galilean clothes.

Albert Schweitzer. Among those who felt that something was wrong was Albert Schweitzer. In the years before he became a medical missionary in West Africa Schweitzer made a massive study of the course of research on the life of Jesus. It earned him a doctorate in theology from the University of Strasbourg and established his reputation as an international scholar. Schweitzer published the results of his research in *The Quest of the Historical Jesus* (1906). Few doctoral dissertations have matched Schweitzer's insight, clarity, and sheer verve. Schweitzer conducts his readers along the highways and byways of German scholarship. At the end of the book he confronts them with a choice. They must choose between thoroughgoing skepticism or Schweitzer's own solution.

To Schweitzer the alternative to thoroughgoing skepticism was thoroughgoing eschatology. It meant realizing that when Jesus talked about the Kingdom of God, he was not simply talking about a program of social reform. The Kingdom of God was a reality that Jesus believed in. It was the reign of God in the end time. Jesus was convinced that his mission in life was to bring this about, even though it meant sacrificing his life for it. It was all bound up with Jewish apocalyptic ideas. But, as Schweitzer insisted, we cannot have Jesus without his apocalyptic ideas. They are the key to understanding the historical Jesus. If we ignore them, we cannot have a historical Jesus at all.

But what Albert Schweitzer appeared to give with one hand he took away with the other. He gave his readers an assurance that many things described in the Gospels happened pretty much as they are described. He gave them Jesus as a solid historical figure. But he took away much of the ground for believing in him. For the Jesus that Schweitzer gave was a Jesus whose head was filled with the obsolete ideas of his times. Jesus actually believed in the imminent coming of the Kingdom of God. But Jesus was wrong. The Kingdom did not come in the way Jesus had expected. And he lost his life in the process.

Schweitzer's Jesus was not a sublime teacher but an imperious ruler. Jesus really did think of himself as the Messiah, the apocalyptic Son of Man and Son of God. But these terms belong to a world that is gone forever. For Schweitzer they could be only "historical parables." Schweitzer himself no more believed in the eschatological world of the New Testament than a modern skeptic would. But this in turn raised the question "Could Jesus himself really be sane and still believe all these things?" It was a question Schweitzer himself tried to answer in the book for which he was awarded his medical degree, *The Psychiatric Study of Jesus.*

In the meantime Schweitzer completed his historical research with the confession that Jesus comes to us "as One unknown, without a name, as of old, by the lake-side, He came to those who knew Him not." He repeats the command "Follow thou me!" And those who obey and perform the tasks that he sets them "shall learn in their own experience Who He is." It was on this mystical, existential note that Schweitzer closed *The Quest of the Historical Jesus.* It was in this spirit that Albert Schweitzer embarked on his career as a jungle doctor.

To many people Schweitzer appeared to have said all that could reasonably be said on the matter. He had certainly given the deathblow to the Jesus of liberal Protestantism. But Schweitzer's alternative Jesus was both uncongenial and elusive. Nor was Schweitzer's version of Christianity the only candidate in the field.

The History of Religions School. The years between 1880 and 1920 saw the heyday of the History of Religions School. The members of this school believed that Christianity should be seen like any other religion against the background of its times. Christianity was one religion among all the other religions of Egypt, Babylonia, Palestine, and the Hellenistic world. Like all other religions, it was to be seen as the product of its cultural background. Many of its beliefs were drawn from that background and have no more claim to validity today than the background itself has.

A typical product of the History of Religions School was Wilhelm Bousset's *Kyrios Christos* (1913). Bousset argued that the idea of Christ's divinity was really derived from pagan religion. In Hellenistic religion the divinities were called "Lords," and the early church had simply copied the practice.

In the same way, miracle stories from the ancient world provided the source and inspiration for the miracle stories concerning Jesus.

Subsequent scholarship has not vindicated Bousset's claims, but certain segments of the academic world continue to be fascinated with the suggested parallels between Jesus and the "divine men" of antiquity. From the time of the English Deists through the nineteenth century and down to the present, someone or other has always argued that Jesus was just another holy man like Apollonius of Tyana who is said to have performed miracles and called people to moral reformation. Beneath the comparison lies the suggestion that neither Jesus nor Apollonius really performed miracles. The stories were just two forms of primitive religious belief.

Barth and Neoorthodoxy. Bousset and the History of Religions School seemed to leave some room for a historical Jesus but not much for a Christ. With Karl Barth it was almost the other way around. To Bousset so many of the ideas associated with Christology came from non-Christian sources that they could be explained away. With Karl Barth it was exactly the opposite. The great failure of liberalism, said Barth, was due to its preoccupation with man and religion and its neglect of God. To a world devastated by two world wars and the Great Depression and haunted by the fear of a nuclear holocaust, Barth proclaimed that God still spoke through his Word.

In the strictest sense of the term, Jesus Christ, said Barth, is God's Word to man. The Bible is the witness to that God. Barth thought of the Bible as witness in the sense of Jesus' words: " 'He who receives you receives me, and he who receives me receives him who sent me' " (Matthew 11:40). Truly to receive in faith and obedience the words of the inspired witnesses to Christ is to receive him, and to receive him is to receive him who sent him, but what interested Barth was not questions concerning the historical Jesus but the implications of Christology.

The Challenge of Bultmann. In some ways Rudolf Bultmann could also be said to have been concerned with the Word of God. But he combined it with a skepticism concerning the historical value of the Gospel accounts and a view of mythology that he inherited from the History of Religions School. To Bultmann the entire thought-world of the New Testament was mythological. He could not believe in angels and demons, heaven and hell, the fall of mankind and redemption by a heavenly redeemer. All these ideas were derived, in his view, from the mythical worlds of Jewish apocalyptic and gnosticism. But like Schweitzer and Bousset, Bultmann dismissed them as obsolete and untenable. What we must do, said Bultmann, is to demythologize the gospel and proclaim an existential form of Christianity. In the process he threw overboard all the miracle stories, which he believed had come into the New Testament from the pagan religions of the ancient world. The upshot was that Bultmann believed that we could be sure *that* Jesus had lived, but we could not know *what* he was really like.

CONTEMPORARY ALTERNATIVES

This kind of skepticism was further reinforced by the publication of *The Myth of God Incarnate* (1977), edited by John Hick. The authors of the book differed among themselves over many points of detail. When they talked about "myth," the reader was left wondering whether they all meant the same thing. But their combined efforts left the general impression that faith was all very difficult, and that the one thing they wanted to discourage their readers from believing was the idea that God had become incarnate in Jesus.

Among the other notable books of the 1970s were two fascinating and contradictory accounts of Jesus and his miracles. Morton Smith, the well-known historian of the ancient world, published a book entitled *Jesus the Magician* (1978). In it Professor Smith revived the old charge that Jesus was really a rather discreditable figure who dabbled in magic. Drawing on various late traditions and mystical papyri, Smith argued that the Gospel accounts of Jesus are really a cover-up, designed to conceal the real facts about Jesus.

On the other hand, the Oxford Jewish scholar Geza Vermes told a very different story in his book *Jesus the Jew* (1973). Vermes saw Jesus as a Galilean charismatic—a type familiar from Jewish writings of the period. Jesus was really a well-intentioned charismatic of a type that flourished in Galilee to the annoyance of the staid and formal members of the Jewish hierarchy in Jerusalem.

Who is right in all this? Clearly they cannot all be right. How do we decide? Where do we go from here?

WHERE DO WE GO FROM HERE?

The ordinary person may simply feel like giving up. In fact, so do many of the experts. They could give up on religion and Christianity. Or they could give up on the world of scholarship. Or they could give up on both.

But if we give up on religion and Christianity, we would just be giving up on the one thing that life is really all about. To turn our backs on God and Jesus would just be the biggest and most expensive mistake we could ever make. In the language of the Bible, we would end up gaining the world and losing ourselves.

And what about the world of scholarship? The layperson is tempted to think that scholars spend their lives knocking down each other's theories. It often looks as if the new ideas of one generation are just the rehashed ideas of the previous generation. Nineteenth-century views of myth have gone. And now twentieth-century scholars are talking about myth again. The twentieth-century scholar laughs at the Victorian portrait of Jesus as a Victorian idealist in Galilean garb. It is just like that of Harnack looking down the well and seeing his own reflection. But the twentieth-century picture of Jesus as "the man for others" simply looks like another version of the same thing.

All too often we seem to be put in a no-win situation. Some scholars offer us a Jesus who is remarkably like themselves, or at least a personification of the ideals that happen to be favored and fashionable at the time. And so we are back to the picture of the scholar seeing only his own reflection. But other scholars look down the well and say, "The well is too deep and the water is too murky to see anything at all." Finally, there are those, like Morton Smith and Geza Vermes, who come up with a picture of Jesus that challenges our accepted ideas.

What do we make of it? If we turn our backs on history and historical research, we run the risk of turning faith into make-believe. Two things could happen. On the one hand, we could end up with a faith that is detached from reality. It would be a faith in a Jesus of our imaginations. It would be a faith in the *un*historical Jesus. On the other hand, we might continue to be devout and faithful, but always fearful of the world of scholarship, always afraid something might come up that would overthrow everything. It would be like living in dread of cancer but deciding that the only way to cope with it is to pretend it does not exist.

But neither of these options is realistic and honest for us today. We cannot simply run away. The alternative is to look fairly and squarely at the issues. When we do this, we shall see that not all scholarship is negative and threatening. The critics we have looked at in this chapter are not necessarily typical of all scholars. They represent a cross-section of those who have challenged the orthodox picture of Jesus in the last two hundred years.

What's the alternative? What are we to make of the Bible's picture of Jesus the miracle worker? I shall give my own answer in Chapter 8–11.

8 / Unscrambling the Puzzle

You see it's like a portmanteau —there are two mean-
ings packed into one word. (Lewis Carroll, *Through*
the Looking-Glass, chapter 5)

I spent much of my school life during the Second World War.
Back in England in those long winter evenings one of my
favorite pastimes was to do jigsaw puzzles. Sometimes I found
that I nearly had the picture finished only to discover that I
had a hole that none of the remaining pieces seemed to fit.
At the same time I had a pile of pieces that seemed to fit
nowhere. There was nothing to do but to look at the picture
more closely to see whether the picture really fitted and made
sense. Looking closer I would see that I had forced some
pieces together that really did not fit. The result was not
surprising. All I could do was to unscramble the parts of the
picture that really did not fit, and put them together in a way
that really fitted.

We often do the same thing with the miracle stories of
the New Testament. We put together a picture that does not
quite fit. And then we discover that we have a lot of pieces
left over that don't seem to fit anywhere. We read into terms
meanings that we feel are obvious, but somehow the picture
that we get looks contrived and forced. We use arguments
that seem to make some sense to us, but somehow they are
not quite the same as those used in the New Testament itself.
We draw conclusions, but the conclusions seem a bit different
from those of the New Testament writers.

Perhaps deep down we feel that something has gone

wrong somewhere. In that case the only way out is to unscramble part of the picture and see if we can put it together in a way that makes better sense and that uses the pieces we had no real use for before. Take the claim that is sometimes made: "Miracles prove the divinity of Christ." A variant of this is the claim: "Jesus was able to do miracles because he was the divine Son of God." We feel that we ought to be able to justify these claims by proof-texting them from the New Testament. But when we actually look at the New Testament, the picture there turns out to be more complex. Some of it may appear at first sight to be downright disconcerting. What we need to avoid is reading our own meanings into the New Testament and then, in turn, trying to justify our meanings from the New Testament. What we need to do is to start with the New Testament and follow its lead.

TWO EXAMPLES OF EARLY PREACHING

The Acts of the Apostles contains a number of summaries of early Christian preaching. The first of these is an account of what Peter said at Pentecost. Here he summed up the activity of Jesus in these terms.

> "Men of Israel, hear these words: Jesus of Nazareth, a man attested to you by God with mighty works and wonders and signs which God did through him in your midst, as you yourselves know. . . " (Acts 2:22)

When Peter proclaimed the gospel to Cornelius and his friends, the first Gentile converts, he preached in a similar strain.

> "You know the word which he sent to Israel, preaching good news of peace by Jesus Christ (he is Lord of all), the word which was proclaimed throughout all Judea, beginning from Galilee after the baptism which John preached: how God anointed Jesus of Nazareth with the Holy Spirit and power; how he went about doing good and healing all that were oppressed by the devil, for God was with him." (Acts 10:36-38)

These descriptions of the ministry of Jesus occur in two key sermons, delivered at crucial phases in the life of the church. The first was when the church was opened up to the Jews at Pentecost. The second was when the church was opened up to the Gentiles. In both cases the Spirit was poured out upon those who received the message.

My point here is certainly not to deny the divinity of Jesus Christ. It is rather to note just how the New Testament approaches his person and to try to grasp how the miracles of Jesus fit into the picture. At first sight these passages seem to be saying rather less than Christians want to say. Jesus' miracles are given a prominent place, but they are not attributed to Jesus as the Second Person of the Trinity. They are not presented as manifestations of his personal divinity. In both passages Jesus is clearly a man. To be precise, he is identified as "Jesus of Nazareth." The stress falls on what "God did through him" (Acts 2:22) and on God being "with him" (Acts 10:38). More precisely still, the latter passage presents Jesus' healing work in the context of God's anointing of him "with the Holy Spirit and power."

In other words, these examples of early Christian preaching do not move directly from the miracles of Jesus to his divinity. They speak about God (i.e., the Father) and the Holy Spirit. When we look at the Gospels to see how they present the miracles of Jesus in relation to the question of his identity, we get the same basic picture, only considerably more filled out. All this suggests that we need to unscramble the picture put together by traditional apologetics of Jesus the divine Son of God, doing the miracles in his own right, as it were. For this is not quite the picture painted by the New Testament. Moreover, it leaves to one side a whole heap of pieces that attribute the miracles sometimes to the Father and sometimes to the Holy Spirit. What I am suggesting is not to deny the incarnation. Rather, it is to examine just how the New Testament gets to the incarnation. It is to say that we need to see both the miracles of Jesus and the question of his person in the context of the Trinity.

WHAT ARE THE TITLES OF JESUS REALLY SAYING?

Son of God. We cannot without more ado assume that the title "Son of God" presents a self-evident rationale for the miracles of Jesus. Although at first sight it might look so to us, the title "Son of God" is not in and of itself a divine title. The title "Son of God" was one that could be applied to the whole nation of Israel. Yahweh addressed Israel as "my son" (Hosea 11:1). And in a special way the kings of Israel were addressed as God's sons. God gave the promise to King David concerning his yet unborn son: "I will be his father, and he shall be my son" (2 Samuel 7:14). This prophecy is repeated in a collection of prophecies at Qumran.

The king is designated as God's son in Psalm 2:7. This Psalm is a royal Psalm. It speaks of God's anointed ruler whom he has set on Zion, God's holy hill, whose heritage is the nations of the earth. The Psalm was used at the enthronement of the kings of Israel. But it is also quoted in the New Testament in several key places (Acts 13:33; Hebrews 1:5; 5:5; 2 Peter 1:17).

The Psalm provides the source for the identification of Jesus with God's Son by the voice from heaven after his baptism and the descent of the Spirit (Matthew 3:17; Mark 1:11; Luke 3:22; cf. John 1:34). The voice from heaven also identifies Jesus with God's beloved in whom he delights. This further identifies Jesus with God's servant upon whom he has put his Spirit (Isaiah 42:1). In other words, "Son of God" is a title of Jesus' messianic kingship, for which Jesus has been anointed by the Spirit.

Luke traces the genealogy of Jesus back to Adam, the son of God (Luke 3:38). No one would dream of claiming the divinity of Adam on these grounds. What the title would have suggested to devout Jews as they read the Scriptures was not divinity but kingship. This was doubtless the meaning that the title would have held for people in Jesus' day. At his trial Jesus was asked by the high priest, "Are you the Christ, the Son of the Blessed?" (Mark 14:61; cf. Matthew 26:63; Luke 22:67). The high priest used the expression "Son of the Blessed" in order to avoid profaning the divine name. He was not asking Jesus whether he was the Second Person of the Trinity. He was asking Jesus whether he was the messianic king.

The reply that Jesus gave to this question is illuminating. For it sheds light on the meaning of three important titles of Jesus: "Son of God," "Christ," and "Son of Man." Jesus replied, " 'I am; and you will see the Son of man sitting at the right hand of Power, and coming with the clouds of heaven' " (Mark 14:62). The question and answer link the three titles together.

It is an oversimplification to say that "Son of God" expresses Jesus' divinity and "Son of Man" expresses his humanity. In and of itself "Son of God" is a title of kingship. As such, it actually expresses humanity. For only human beings could be sons of God in this sense. The same goes for Adam. As son of God, he was, as it were, the king of the earth. What Jesus did was to redefine the title and fill it with a new significance.

Son of Man. In a curious sort of way the title "Son of Man" points in the same direction as "Son of God." Several elements are in the background. The name Adam is the generic term for man. So the title "Son of Man" carries with it the idea of the Son of Adam. What Adam was meant to do and be, but failed, Jesus did and was. But other elements are in the background as well. The reply of Jesus to the high priest takes up the theme of Daniel 7:13. In this vision "one like a son of man" is presented before the Ancient of Days and is given everlasting dominion. All peoples will serve him. Scholars debate heatedly the identity of the figure in Daniel. Some say that he embodies the saints of the Most High (Daniel 7:18). Others say that he is an angelic figure. Still others say that he represents the true Israelite, the guardian of the people, the one who has remained faithful and loyal to God in the face of great hostility and persecution.

One of the interesting things about Jesus' teaching is the way in which he spoke about "*the* Son of Man." In my view, the best explanation for this is that he saw the title as a vocation. It was a kind of job description. It is as if he were saying, "It is my vocation to be the Son of Man—the one that the Book of Daniel describes." If the figure in Daniel is a human figure, it is as if Jesus is saying, "It is my vocation to fulfil the calling to be the Son of Man described by Daniel— the true righteous Israelite who remains faithful to God despite all opposition." If the figure in Daniel is an angelic being, it may be that Jesus was saying in effect, "It is not an angel who is the true Son of Man, but I!" (This may well explain why the Epistle to the Hebrews is at pains to distinguish between Jesus as the Son and the angels in its opening chapters. The point may be to put readers straight that it is not an angel who has achieved redemption, but Jesus the Son.)

The title "Son of Man" certainly draws attention to the humanity of Jesus. But it also carries with it the idea of God's special representative. The prophet Ezekiel was addressed by God as "Son of man." As such, he was summoned to represent God to the people of Israel (Ezekiel 2:3; 3:4-11). He was called upon to consume the word of God and utter it to the people, whether they heard or refused to hear (Ezekiel 3:1-11; cf. Matthew 4:4). He was called to bear the punishment of the people (Ezekiel 4:4). He was filled with the Spirit (Ezekiel 2:2; 3:12, 14, 24).

In these various ways these images of the Son of Man anticipate Jesus as the Son of Man, God's faithful, righteous representative, the true heir of Adam, the true man, the one who will reign in righteousness and inherit the earth.

Christ. The title "Christ" also deserves careful attention. It does not simply mean the coming one, the expected deliverer, the messianic king who would overthrow the enemies of God's people and reign in righteousness. The title "Christ" comes from the Greek word *Christos*, which in turn translates the Hebrew word *māšíaḥ* (messiah). Both the Greek and the Hebrew words mean "anointed." But this raises the question "Anointed with what?" Priests and kings in the Old Testament were anointed with oil. But Jesus was anointed by the Holy Spirit after his baptism. As we saw earlier, this is a point that Peter was at pains to make in his preaching to Cornelius and his companions (Acts 10:38). We shall follow it up in the next chapter. In the meantime, we need to underline a point that is often overlooked. When the title "Christ" is applied to Jesus, it carries with it an implicit reference to the Holy Spirit. When people confess Jesus as the Christ, they are not simply confessing Jesus as (to use the language of later theology) the Second Person of the Trinity. They are confessing him in his divinely appointed role, and they are also confessing the Spirit as the one who anointed him for this role and who enabled him to fulfil this role.

All this may seem to have taken us some way from the question of miracles. But there is a good reason for this detour. In order to appreciate the miracle stories of the Gospels, we need to see what the Gospel writers meant and how the miracles fit into the total picture that they paint.

MIRACLES AND TRUTH CLAIMS

Let us now turn to the place of miracles in Christian apologetics and the part they play in the truth claims that are made for the Christian faith. In the past, miracles have been seen as proof of the truth of Christian claims. Since miracles were acts that only God could do, miracles authenticated the truth of the Christian revelation. Some theologians have even argued that miracles were given in order to establish the canon of Scripture. Once the canon was fixed, there was no further need of miracles. But there is little to be said for this argument. Nowhere in the New Testament are miracles bound up with the inspiration of Scripture and the identification of certain writings as inspired Scripture.

But what about the Gospel miracles? Don't they attest Jesus in some way? At Pentecost Peter left his hearers in no doubt. He told them that Jesus of Nazareth was " 'a man attested to you by God with mighty works and wonders and signs which God did through him in your midst, as you yourselves know' " (Acts 2:22). John's Gospel makes a similar point when it records Jesus' charge against his opponents: " 'If I had not done among them the works which no one else did, they would not have sin; but now they have seen and hated both me and my Father' " (John 15:24).

But what exactly are these passages saying? They are saying that the works of Jesus were works that only God could do. They are also saying that the people to whom these words were addressed had actually seen them for themselves. Under these circumstances the inferences were inescapable. The works of Jesus demanded a positive response to Jesus from those who witnessed them. His works were the works of God himself. Refusing to recognize this would only proceed from sinful obstinacy. A negative response could only be sinful.

Miracles and Proof. Do the New Testament miracles mean that the miracle stories have the same compelling, evidential force for us today? Some Christian writers definitely think so. They argue that if they had that force then, they must have the same force today. But two things need to be remembered.

The first thing to be remembered is the difference between an event and a report of the event. If it is one thing to see an event for oneself, it is another to read a report of the event. John 9 tells the story of how Jesus restored the sight of a man who was born blind. Some of the Jews doubted whether the man was really born blind or whether the man who could now see was the same man who was born blind. But they were able to check this out by asking the man's parents. The eyewitnesses were in a position to test the claims personally. But we are not. The same goes for Peter's preaching. Peter was appealing to what the onlookers had seen for themselves. But we do not have this direct access to the events in question. We have only *reports* of the events. All that we can do is to test the general trustworthiness of the *report* and then decide whether to believe particular items contained in the report. And with this we are brought back again to the arguments of the previous chapter. The decision to believe or reject the miracle stories of the Gospels is bound up with our broader view of reality and the feasibility of miracles within it (in other words, with what we called our frame of reference). And this in turn affects the way we look at the Gospels themselves as historical accounts.

What we cannot do is to appeal to the miracle stories as compelling, objective evidence for the divine inspiration of Scripture and at the same time to appeal to the inspiration of Scripture as the ground of our claim for the historicity of the miracle stories.

Is there any way out of the dilemma? Perhaps at this point we need to remind ourselves of the issue at stake. The question is not simply whether this or that miracle actually happened as described; it is whether this or that miracle *can be shown to have happened.* Some Christian writers talk in broad terms about demonstrating the historicity of miracles. But when it comes to the point, they do not argue for the historicity of any particular miracle reported to have been performed by Jesus. They go straight to the resurrection of Jesus. If the resurrection can be shown to have been a historical event, then at least the other lesser miracles are more feasible.

MIRACLES AND THE RESURRECTION

But What Does the Resurrection of Jesus Prove? Once more we need to unscramble the puzzle and put it together the way the New Testament writers put it together. First of all, we need to look at two arguments the biblical writers do not use themselves.

The first argument says in effect, "I grant that I cannot prove that every single miracle story happened exactly as described, for many of them lack objective, corroborating evidence. But I can show that the resurrection of Jesus was a historical event. And if God can pull off something as difficult as bringing someone back to life from the dead, he could easily have pulled off the lesser miracles."

The second argument can be put like this. "The resurrection of Jesus proves his personal divinity. If he was God, he could have done all the things that he is said to have done."

Granted, I have put these arguments in their crudest, starkest form. I have done so in order to bring out their thrust. The point to be grasped is that the New Testament writers do not, in fact, argue along these lines. For one thing they do not narrow down their argument to the historicity of the resurrection, and then make a vague appeal to the feasibility of the other miracles in the light of it. Peter appealed (as we have seen) to the works of Jesus in general, which were there for all to see already before the resurrection. In a similar vein John rounds off his account of Jesus' ministry with the words: "Now Jesus did many other signs in the presence of the disciples, which are not written in this book; but these are written that you may believe that Jesus is the Christ, the Son of God, and that believing you may have life in his name" (John 20:30-31).

The resurrection of Jesus is certainly presented in the New Testament as a historical event. The four Gospels give accounts of the appearances of the risen Christ to various followers. It was the basis of the church's faith and indeed of its very existence (1 Corinthians 15:3-19). If Christ has not been raised, the Christian faith is futile. This argument of the apostle Paul is not an argument from *what may be* to *what must be*, or from necessity to fact. It is, rather, a stark recognition of the futility of Christianity if Christ has not been raised from the dead.

It has become fashionable in some theological circles to say that the last fact available to the historian is the Easter faith of the disciples. In other words, we know beyond all reasonable doubt that the early church *believed* that Jesus was raised from the dead. This is a fact to which we have access. But what lay behind that fact remains hidden from us. I do not think, however, that we can remain content with this argument.

Admittedly, no one saw the resurrection taking place. What people claim to have seen was the risen Christ. But we cannot stop simply with the Easter faith of the first Christians. For history cannot admit causeless events. The historian is not simply concerned with dates and data. The goal is always to try to get behind the dates and the data to the *explanation* that accounts for them. The historian has to ask how and why the Easter faith came into being in the first place. Why did Jesus not remain a martyred hero, like some of the figures in the Old Testament or like Socrates in Greek history? Why would the early Christians invent such an improbable story and risk their lives for it, if there were not something real behind it?

History, science, and theology have this in common, that they all have to do with discovering and defending explanations. My late teacher, Alan Richardson, saw this very clearly. In the preface of his *Introduction to the Theology of the New Testament* he confessed that in his book

> the hypothesis is defended that Jesus himself is the author of the brilliant re-interpretation of the Old Testament scheme of salvation ('Old Testament theology') which is found in the New Testament, and that the events of the life, 'signs',

> passion and resurrection of Jesus, as attested by the apostolic witness, can account for the 'data' of the New Testament better than any other hypothesis current today. It makes better 'sense', or better history, than, for instance, the hypothesis that St. Paul (or someone else) transformed the simple ethical monotheism of a young Jewish carpenter-rabbi into a new mystery-religion of the dying-and-rising-god pattern with the crucified rabbi as its cult-hero. (*An Introduction to the Theology of the New Testament* [London: SCM Press, 1958], p. 12)

Although these words were written nearly a generation ago, they still hold true. The resurrection of Jesus is the one necessary explanation of the existence of the Christian church and its faith.

The Resurrection of Jesus in the New Testament. When we look at what the New Testament writers actually say about the resurrection of Jesus, we discover that they do not argue like some of the church fathers. They do not say, "The resurrection proves the personal divinity of Jesus because being God he could not die." In general, the New Testament writers speak of Jesus being raised from the dead or being raised by the Father (e.g., Acts 2:24; 4:10; 10:40; 1 Corinthians 15:4, 12-14, 20, 23, 38; Galatians 1:1; Hebrews 13:20). Paul could even attribute the resurrection to the Spirit of holiness (Romans 1:4). The New Testament does not say that Jesus raised himself. Perhaps the nearest that it comes to saying this is in John 2:19. But even here it should be remembered that it is the Father who is speaking through Jesus (John 8:28, 38; 12:49-50; 14:10; 17:8). Moreover, John 2:22 reverts to the passive language of Jesus being raised from the dead. Similarly, the "power" referred to in John 10:18 is given by the Father.

The point of this whole line of argument is this. In the New Testament the resurrection of Jesus is not simply his restoration to life. It is also the reversal of the verdict and the sentence that was pronounced on him. In terms of Jewish law the only construction that could be placed on his death was that he was under the curse of God (Galatians 3:13; cf. Deuteronomy 21:23). The slogan "Jesus be cursed!" (1 Corinthians 12:3) probably represents the official Jewish attitude on how Jesus should be regarded by orthodox Jews. Jesus was condemned as a blasphemer with messianic pretensions who was trying to lead the people astray (Matthew 28:63-66; Mark 14:64-65; John 11:47-53).

The miracles of Jesus play an important part in the decision to liquidate him. The Jewish leaders saw them as occult practices designed to lead the people away from God. Profanation of the sabbath was one thing. It was punishable by excommunication. But witchcraft, sorcery, and presumptuous false prophecy were something else. They were punishable by death (Exodus 22:18; Deuteronomy 18:10-12). The practitioner of signs and wonders who led the people astray was to be put to death so that the evil might be purged from the midst of the people (Deuteronomy 13:1-15). In short, the Jewish leaders saw Jesus as someone who was performing signs and wonders in order to get a following for his false teaching and practices. If this is so, the resurrection takes on a new meaning. It represents the Father's verdict on Jesus his Son, which reverses the verdict of the Jewish hierarchy. As such, it is an endorsement of the works of Jesus, making it clear that they are not works of sorcery punishable by death, but truly the works of God. Jesus was not a false prophet or sorcerer, but the one whom God would raise up in the end time who would speak in God's name (Acts 3:22-23; 7:37; cf. Deuteronomy 18:15-19; John 6:14). The resurrection tells us that the one who raised Jesus is the one who was working in him all along.

PROOFS AND SIGNS

One part of the picture still needs some unscrambling. It has to do with the difference between a sign and a proof. Signs and proofs are not the same thing. When I drive along the freeway and see a green sign that reads "Pasadena—Next Eleven Exits," I am not being treated to a logical demonstration that each and all of the next eleven off ramps will lead me to Pasadena. I am being given a pointer. Only in following the directions of the sign do I discover whether the sign is telling the truth or not. After all, someone could have planted the signs with the deliberate intention of leading people astray. The function of a sign is to point beyond itself. It has meaning and truth only as it fulfils its function within the context of the sign language that it employs.

This last point applies to the miracles of Jesus as "signs" no less than road signs. As we saw in the last chapter, one of the characteristic biblical words for a miracle was the word "sign." But in the Bible miraculous signs do not have a purely external function. They do not function like an external proof or guarantee that what is being said has the divine stamp of approval on it. The signs themselves are actually part of the message.

All too often in the past Christian apologists have been so preoccupied with the miraculous as divine authentication of Christian beliefs that they have neglected what the signs themselves might be saying. For centuries prophets had performed signs. Such signs did not have to be miraculous. Nor were they something external to the message. In fact, they illustrated and embodied the message. The prophet Isaiah went around naked as a sign of the coming desolation (Isaiah 20:2-3). Hosea married a harlot (Hosea 1:2-3). Jeremiah wore a yoke as a sign to the people of their coming bondage (Jeremiah 27–28). Ezekiel prophesied the union of Judah and Ephraim by joining two sticks (Ezekiel 37:15-23). In New Testament times John the Baptist dressed in the traditional likeness of Elijah, the expected forerunner of the day of the Lord (Mark 1:6; cf. 2 Kings 1:8). The Christian prophet bound his own hands and feet with Paul's girdle as a sign of Paul's captivity (Acts 21:10-11).

Jesus himself stood in this tradition and used symbolic

acts to illustrate and embody his teaching. His action of taking a child into his arms embodied and exemplified the Father's love (Mark 9:36; cf. 10:13-16). He instructed his disciples to shake the dust off their feet as a testimony to the unbelieving cities (Mark 6:11). He dramatized his messiahship by riding into Jerusalem in the manner of the prophecy of Zechariah 9:9. Jesus' action in washing his disciples' feet (John 13:1-20) was likewise such a sign. Such signs were like acted parables. They were not external to the message but the embodiment of it. In the same way baptism and the Lord's Supper are to be seen in the tradition of prophetic signs.

It is in this tradition—or, to use the expression that we have earlier used, this *frame of reference*—that we can best appreciate the miracle stories of the Gospels. The miracle stories do not function as external proofs of the truth of the message. They are part of the message itself. They are an embodiment of the message. They are like acted parables. They have a story to tell. They confront us as signs that point beyond themselves to the one who performs them. To read them correctly, we need to understand the sign language to which they belong.

9 / Remaking the Puzzle

Step 1: Mark's Picture of Jesus

A moment's insight is sometimes worth a life's experience. (Oliver Wendell Holmes, *The Professor at the Breakfast Table*, chapter 10)

We can get very set in our ways. We can look at something for years and years and simply take it for granted. It is so familiar that we fail to grasp its significance. We can do this with the Gospel stories about Jesus. We are so accustomed to the experiences of a lifetime that we sometimes miss the point of what is being said. The Gospel stories themselves are full of incidents about people who were doing the very same thing. They were set in their ways. They had a lifetime's experience behind them. And they had closed minds. They were not ready for anything new. But the Gospel stories also tell of others who got insights that were indeed worth more than a lifetime's experience. In some cases the experiences of a lifetime were leading them up to their great moment of insight.

We have now come to the point where we can look at what the four Gospels are actually saying about Jesus and his miracles. Mark's Gospel is the shortest of the four New Testament accounts of Jesus' life and ministry. Most scholars (myself included) think that it was the first account of Jesus to be written down. Matthew and Luke follow the same broad outline that Mark follows, but supplement Mark in significant ways. John gives an independent perspective. But before we look at the Gospels, we need to look at two neglected factors that have repeatedly been overlooked in trying to understand what is going on in the Gospels.

We shall approach the task of remaking the puzzle in three steps. In Step 1 we shall piece together what Mark says about Jesus in the light of the two neglected factors that I have just mentioned. In Step 2 we shall piece together what Matthew, Luke, and John have to say. And in Step 3 we shall consider the emerging picture of Jesus. My aim in these next three chapters is to give an overview of what the four Gospels are saying about Jesus and to ask how miracles fit into the picture. At the same time I am asking, "What does this picture tell us about Jesus and about God?"

TWO NEGLECTED FACTORS

Baptism with the Holy Spirit. The first neglected factor is the prophecy of John the Baptist which in one form or another is recorded in all four Gospels. Mark's Gospel records it in this form: " 'I have baptized you with water; but he will baptize you with the Holy Spirit' " (Mark 1:8; cf. Matthew 3:11; Luke 3:16; John 1:33). Broadly speaking, there are three main lines of interpretation concerning this prophecy of baptism with the Holy Spirit. In traditional Catholic theology, the baptism of the Holy Spirit is linked with the rite of baptism. In Reformed Protestant theology, it is linked with the gift of the Spirit in regeneration, conversion, and justification by faith. In Pentecostal and charismatic theology, baptism with the Holy Spirit is linked with postconversion experiences of grace and gifts for Christian service.

The trouble with all three lines of interpretation is that they miss the point of what is being said here in the four Gospels. For they tend to jump straight from John the Baptist's prophecy to the outpouring of the Spirit at Pentecost and fail to see its relevance for the ministry of Jesus in his lifetime. In practice they treat the ministry of Jesus as an interlude between the prophecy and the outpouring of the Spirit at Pentecost. In so doing they treat this prophecy as if it were the same as Acts 1:5 and Acts 11:16.

To grasp the point, we need to ask ourselves: "Who is saying what to whom?" In the prophecy recorded in Acts 1:5 and 11:16 the Lord is speaking to the disciples about the baptism of the Holy Spirit that they themselves will receive. But in the four Gospels John the Baptist is addressing those Jews from Judea and Jerusalem who have come to him for baptism. It is they who in his prophecy will be baptized by the coming one with the Holy Spirit.

I am not denying the activity of the Spirit in conversion, baptism, and the giving of spiritual gifts. Nor am I attempting to undercut the discussion between Catholic, Reformed, and Pentecostal charismatic Christians concerning the baptism with the Holy Spirit. My point is rather that we must discuss the post-Pentecost Christian experience of the baptism of the Holy Spirit against the background of the baptism of the Holy Spirit that went on in the actual ministry of Jesus himself.

It is sometimes said that there was no ministry of the Spirit until Pentecost. In support of this view, appeal is made to the invitation recorded in John's Gospel to come to Jesus and drink with the accompanying promise, " ' "Out of his heart shall flow rivers of living water" ' " (John 7:38). John adds the comment: "Now this he said about the Spirit, which those who believed in him were to receive; for as yet the Spirit had not yet been given, because Jesus was not yet glorified" (John 7:39). But to say that there was no activity of the Spirit in Jesus' ministry is to ignore the many references to the Spirit in the Gospels' account of his ministry. And it is also to misread this passage. For the point of the passage is not to deny all activity of the Spirit prior to the glorification of Jesus, but to say that the Spirit was not yet given *in the manner described in the passage* to those who were to receive it.

If we jump to the conclusion that Mark 1:8 and its parallels refer directly to Pentecost and have no real relevance to the ministry of Jesus, we shall miss the full significance of a lot of what is being said in the Gospels. The four Gospels themselves do not include an account of Pentecost. But all four record the prophecy up front in their accounts of Jesus. I would go so far as to say that their account of what follows is deliberately intended to show how Jesus fulfilled this prophecy. No doubt the four Gospels were written for readers in the post-Pentecost situation. They were written for readers who had either had some experience of the Spirit or who at least had heard of the Holy Spirit in the church. The Gospel accounts are designed to show that Jesus and the Spirit are related, to give a record of Jesus' ministry and the way in which it was received.

If we begin by assuming that baptism with the Holy Spirit is to be equated with speaking in tongues or the possession of particular gifts, we shall be starting at the wrong end. If we do this, it is not surprising that we fail to see any relevance of John's prophecy to the ministry of Jesus. But if we start at the other end and ask what John the Baptist might have meant by baptism, the picture begins to come clearer. Baptism was a symbolic act of washing, cleansing from sin, and consecration. In effect John was saying, "I have washed, cleansed, and consecrated you with water; but he will wash, cleanse, and consecrate you with the Holy Spirit."

The theme of the cleansing and consecration of the people of Israel was closely related to the day of the Lord in prophetic expectation (Isaiah 4:4). The coming of the Spirit in the end time, as the means of cleansing, renewing, and establishing righteousness, is widely attested in the Old Testament (e.g., Isaiah 32:15; 44:3; Ezekiel 18:31; 36:25-29; 37:14; 39:29; Joel 2:28-31; cf. Acts 2:17-21). Some of these passages speak of the outpouring of the Spirit on the nation, as God's servant. Others link the Spirit with wisdom, knowledge, and understanding (e.g., Isaiah 11:2; 40:13-14), while still others speak of the Spirit and the LORD's anointed or the LORD's servant (Isaiah 11:2; 42:1; 48:16; 59:19-21; 61:1).

In addition to these references to the Spirit, we should note what the prophecy of Malachi says concerning the return of the LORD to his temple, the day of his coming, his refining and his purification of the sons of Levi "till they present right offerings to the LORD" (Malachi 3:1-5). The Gospel writers took Malachi's message of the messenger who would prepare the way of the LORD as prophecy that was fulfilled by John the Baptist (Malachi 3:1; Matthew 11:10; Mark 1:2; Luke 1:17, 76; 7:27). He was the Elijah who would come before the great and terrible day of the Lord (Malachi 4:5; Matthew 17:11; Mark 9:12; Luke 1:17). Implicit in this understanding is the identification of Jesus as the one in whom the LORD would return to his temple and refine God's people.

Alongside these biblical passages we should note the expectation of the Qumran Community, which linked the thought of cleansing, instruction, and the Spirit of truth (The Community Rule 4; see G. Vermes, *The Dead Sea Scrolls in English* [Harmondsworth: Pelican Books, 1962], pp. 77-78). The Qumran Community's view of two opposing Spirits is echoed in the Gospels in the contrast between Beelzebul and the Holy Spirit. The Qumran Community looked to the Teacher of Righteousness. The evangelists saw in Jesus the one in whom messianic prophecy was fulfilled and in whom expectation of the Spirit was met. These were not two separate lines of prophecy; they coincided in Jesus. For the messiah was the messiah precisely because he was anointed by the Spirit.

How does all this affect the question of miracles? What I want to suggest and show in the pages that follow is that they play an important part in the way Jesus fulfilled John the Baptist's prophecy that " 'He will baptize you with the Holy Spirit.' " Jesus did this through his teaching, his condemnation of sin, and his renewal of men and women through dealing with their sins and setting them on a new course of life. He did it too through exorcisms, liberation from the powers of evil, and cleansing from sickness and disease. Another way of putting all this is to say that he inaugurated the Kingdom of God—the reign of God. And he did all this as the Son of Man, the Son of God, the Christ, the Servant of the Lord who was anointed by the Spirit to accomplish the Lord's work.

Jewish Attitudes to Wonder Workers Who Lead the People Astray. Before we take a closer look at the Gospels, we need to look briefly at the second of the two neglected factors that I mentioned at the outset. It concerns the special significance of Deuteronomy 13 for understanding what is going on in the Gospels. Scholars and theologians have long been familiar with this passage. It is alluded to in the warning of Jesus against false Christs and false prophets who perform signs and wonders in their attempt to lead the elect astray (Matthew 24:24; Mark 13:22). Spinoza appealed to it to show how little signs and wonders were valued in the Old Testament. Calvin turned to it for an answer on how to deal with Roman Catholic miracles. I commented on it briefly toward the end of the previous chapter.

The passage says that if a prophet arises among the people of God, or a dreamer of dreams, and gives them a sign or a wonder, and if he says "Let us go after other gods," the people are not to go. They are to see it as a test of whether they truly love the LORD their God. Not only are they to pay no heed to such a prophet; they are to kill him because he has taught rebellion against the LORD their God. In killing him they will purge the evil out of the midst of the people.

For Calvin the passage provided ample reason for disregarding miracles in the Catholic church. However impressive the miracle might be, if it was associated with false teaching, it should be disregarded. The point is an important one, and it is still valid today in dealing with reports of signs and wonders, wherever they come from. But the point has a significance that reaches far beyond this. Let us try to put ourselves in the place of an orthodox Pharisee or rabbi, and ask ourselves how we might view Jesus. We might well see him as an upstart, a teacher of new-fangled doctrines, as someone who did not keep the law. We might see him as someone who was trying to get a following and turn people from the established ways. We might see him as someone who was doing (or reported to do) signs and wonders in order to lead the people astray. We might have heard stories about him going into the wilderness and talking with Satan. And then we might ask ourselves, "What should we do about him?" As God-fearing, law-abiding people, we would turn to the Word of God and ask what it says about such a man. The answer of Deuteronomy 13 is quite clear.

> "But that prophet or that dreamer of dreams shall be put to death, because he has taught rebellion against the LORD your God, who brought you out of the land of Egypt and redeemed you out of the house of bondage, to make you leave the way in which the LORD your God commanded you to walk. So you shall purge the evil from the midst of you." (Deuteronomy 13:5)

This passage presents us with a vital key to understanding what is going on in the four Gospels. Further light is shed by Deuteronomy 17 and 18, which contain specific instructions on dealing with transgressors of the covenant, sorcerers, dreamers, wizards, necromancers, and presumptuous false prophets. The scribes, the Pharisees, the priests, and all the rest were not simply jealous of the success of Jesus with the people. They were alarmed at what he was saying and doing. It contradicted generations of tradition. It went against a lifetime's experience. They saw Jesus as a blasphemer and law-breaker long before any question of his messiahship broke upon the public at large. But they saw Jesus through the filter of their own understanding.

The best explanation for his exorcisms and healings that they could come up with was that he was doing all this in the power of Satan. They totally disregarded the self-contradiction at the heart of this charge. They viewed Jesus within a frame of reference supplied by a traditional understanding of the books of the law. They failed to see what the followers of Jesus saw, that the key to understanding Jesus was to be found not only in the law but also in the prophets, the Psalms, and the other writings.

What we have, therefore, are two frames of reference. In the one used by the Jewish leaders of his day Jesus appeared as a blasphemous, false pretender who performed signs and wonders in order to lead the people astray. In the one used by the early church Jesus was the Spirit-anointed Christ, the Son of God, whose works were the work of God himself. Let us now see how all this works out in the stories the Gospels tell us about Jesus.

MARK'S PICTURE OF JESUS

Jesus' Early Ministry. Mark describes his work as "the gospel of Jesus Christ, the Son of God" (Mark 1:1). He begins with an allusion to Malachi 3:1, which (as we have already seen) identifies John the Baptist with the messenger sent to prepare the way of the LORD. A brief description of John's ministry leads to the prophecy of Mark 1:8: " 'I have baptized you with water; but he will baptize you with the Holy Spirit.' " Then follows the account of Jesus' baptism and the descent of the Spirit like a dove. Drawing on Psalm 2:7 and Isaiah 42:1, the voice from heaven declares: " 'Thou art my beloved Son; with thee I am well pleased' " (Mark 1:11). Psalm 2 is a royal Psalm addressing the king as God's son. Isaiah 42 speaks of the servant on whom God has put his Spirit in order to bring justice to the earth.

Baptism is a symbolic act of washing, cleansing, and consecration. It has overtones of being immersed, but the point of the immersion is to wash, cleanse, and consecrate John's baptism recalls the prophetic signs of old. Mark says that he "appeared in the wilderness, preaching a baptism of repentance for the forgiveness of sin" (Mark 1:4). The baptism enacted the message that was preached. But in Jesus' case there was no need of a baptism of repentance. John declared, " 'After me comes he who is mightier than I, the thong of whose sandals I am not worthy to stoop down and untie' " (Mark 1:7). Nevertheless, Jesus came to him for baptism. For Jesus, baptism at the hands of John was an act of consecration. It consecrated him to the service of the penitent sinners with whom he identified himself. It consecrated him as the one of whom John prophesied. This consecration through John's baptism was the necessary step to the anointing by the Spirit that immediately followed and the identification of Jesus by the voice from heaven as the messianic Son of God.

Mark's talk about "a voice from heaven" does not mean that we are forced to think of a voice booming down from the sky. The Jews of Mark's day would have known what the expression meant. It meant a voice from God, for pious Jews often used the word "heaven" in order to avoid profaning the divine name. Matthew's Gospel does this when it uses the expression "kingdom of heaven" instead of "kingdom of God." Moreover, when God spoke to his people in Old Testament times, he spoke through human voices. The word of the LORD came to the prophet so-and-so, and the message that was delivered was spoken through a human voice. The rabbis used the expression *Bath Qol* (Hebrew for "Daughter of a Voice") to denote revelations from God to human beings. With the cessation of Old Testament prophecy the *Bath Qol* remained in rabbinic thought the means of communicating revelations from God. Already Mark 1:3 has spoken of " 'the voice of one crying in the wilderness,' " delivering a message from God. Mark 1:11 delivers another such word from God.

This episode is followed by the brief account of the Spirit driving Jesus into the wilderness where he was tempted by Satan, the arrest of John and the beginning of Jesus' preaching of the Kingdom of God, and the call of the first disciples. The first incident in Jesus' ministry that Mark describes takes place in the synagogue at Capernaum on the sabbath (Mark 1:21-27). Jesus is accosted by a man with an unclean spirit who recognizes Jesus as " 'the Holy One of God.' " Mark presents a contrast between the two spirits: the unclean spirit in the man and the Holy Spirit who has descended upon Jesus and who now leads him. In Jesus' action of driving out the unclean spirit Mark intends us to see how Jesus was now beginning to fulfil John the Baptist's prophecy. It is the first instance of baptizing with the Holy Spirit.

The remainder of Mark 1 is taken up with stories of further healings and exorcisms. It is climaxed with the cleansing of the leper (Mark 1:40-44). In cleansing the man from his leprosy Jesus ordered him to say nothing to anyone, but to show himself to the priest " 'and offer for your cleansing what Moses commanded, for a proof to them.' " This action was in accordance with the requirements of the law (Leviticus 13:49; 14:2-32). It invited the question as to how the man had come to be healed. It was not only a physical healing. It restored the man to his place as a member of the community of God's people.

Mark 2 introduces a further aspect of cleansing—the healing of the paralytic whose prior need is the forgiveness of his sins. Jesus' pronouncement " 'My son, your sins are forgiven' " prompts the question " 'Why does this man speak thus? It is blasphemy! Who can forgive sins but God alone?' " Jesus' response contains the declaration that he has spoken in this way " 'that you may know that the Son of man has authority on earth to forgive sins.' "

The call of Levi and Jesus' action in eating with tax collectors provokes unfavorable comment. To this Jesus replies: " 'Those who are well have no need of a physician, but those who are sick; I came not to call the righteous, but sinners' " (Mark 2:17).

All this cuts across the Pharisees' understanding of correct, godly conduct and true piety. The tension is aggravated by Jesus' defense of his disciples in not fasting, and his sanction of their plucking corn on the sabbath: " 'The sabbath was made for man, not man for the sabbath; so the Son of man is lord even of the sabbath' " (Mark 2:27-28).

Matters come to a head with the healing on the sabbath of the man with a withered hand. Jesus' action in healing the man and the man's act in stretching out his hand could both be construed as work done on the sabbath. The event leads to the decision of the Pharisees to destroy Jesus. Mark's account brings out the ironic contrast between Jesus' action by which the man's hand was "restored" and the Pharisees' action in taking counsel how to "destroy" Jesus. What prompted the action of the Pharisees, who enjoyed a reputation for their piety and devotion? The reason is to be found in the explanation we have given. They saw Jesus as an evil-doer, a blasphemer who was flagrantly undermining the law and leading the people astray with his signs, wonders, and false teaching. The only course open for them was to follow the instructions of Deuteronomy 13 concerning such matters and purge the evil out of their midst.

Mark 3 continues with accounts of more healings and exorcisms and the appointment of the Twelve to whom he gave authority to preach and to cast out demons. Then follows an episode that might be called the anticlimax of Mark's Gospel. It is the negative counterpart to the positive confession at Caesarea Philippi of Jesus as the Christ, which Peter makes later on (Mark 8:27-30). It concerns the charge (one might even say "confession") that Jesus " 'is possessed by Beelzebul, and by the prince of demons he casts out demons' " (Mark 3:22). The conflict with the Pharisees has now come to the boiling point. They now say openly what they have been suspecting for some time. Moreover, if Jesus can be convicted on this charge, the way is clear for his execution, which will purge the evil from their midst.

Jesus' response is to point out the absurdity of this charge: " 'How can Satan cast out Satan?' " (Mark 3:23). If a house or a kingdom is divided against itself, it cannot stand.

If Satan is risen up against himself he cannot stand. His kingdom is coming to an end. The conclusion to be drawn is that Jesus has bound the strong man and is plundering his house. This leads to Jesus' pronouncement on blasphemy and eternal sin.

> "Truly, I say to you, all sins will be forgiven the sons of men, and whatever blasphemies they utter; but whoever blasphemes against the Holy Spirit never has forgiveness, but is guilty of an eternal sin." (Mark 3:28)

It is Jesus' accusers who are the blasphemers. Their blasphemy is not against Jesus as such. It is *blasphemy against the Holy Spirit*. Mark's concluding comment explains the reason: "For they had said, 'He has an unclean spirit' " (Mark 3:30). They had attributed to an unclean spirit what in fact was the work of the Holy Spirit.

This climactic comment reinforces the conclusion that what Jesus was doing he was doing in the power of the Holy Spirit. It strengthens the contention that Mark's account of Jesus' ministry is to be seen as the account of how Jesus fulfilled John the Baptist's prophecy " 'He will baptize you with the Holy Spirit.' " The issue at stake is this: "By what spirit is Jesus acting?" His enemies say that he has an unclean spirit. His followers say that he was anointed by the Holy Spirit.

"Spirit Christology" and "Word Christology." The account that I have given so far might well be called a Spirit Christology. "Christ" means "anointed," and Mark makes it clear that Jesus was anointed by the Spirit as the messianic Son of God after his baptism. In his account of Jesus' activity he calls attention to the role of the Spirit in Jesus' activity. This activity of the Spirit in and through Jesus constitutes the presence of the Kingdom or reign of God. But alongside this emphasis on the Spirit, Mark places an emphasis on the Word. Alongside this explicit Spirit Christology, Mark presents an implicit Word Christology.

Jesus preaches "the gospel of God" (Mark 1:14). He commands the disciples to follow him (Mark 1:17). The unclean spirit is rebuked and exorcised by the word of Jesus' command (Mark 1:15). The people are amazed at the "new teaching" and "authority" of Jesus (Mark 1:27). It is by the word spoken by Jesus that the leper is made clean (Mark 1:41). He declares to the paralytic the word of forgiveness of sins, which only God may speak (Mark 2:5, 7). Jesus' various pronouncements in Mark concerning fellowship with sinners, fasting, new cloth, new wine, and the sabbath are spoken with an authority above that of the scribes. The man with the withered hand is likewise healed by the word of Jesus (Mark 3:5). He gives his disciples authority to preach and cast out demons (Mark 3:14-15). Lest there be any doubt as to what Jesus is doing, the interpretation of the parable of the sower declares that the sower sows the word (Mark 4:14). This parable of the Kingdom is a comment on the audience's reaction to Jesus' ministry so far.

In short, Mark's Spirit Christology is inextricably linked with a Word Christology. Jesus utters the word of God. He speaks as only God himself is entitled to speak. His speech-acts, like the speech-acts of God in the Old Testament, accomplish what is uttered. Together with his activity in the power of the Spirit these speech-acts determine the nature of Jesus' messiahship and sonship.

Nature Miracles. At this point Mark introduces the nature miracles alongside further accounts of exorcism and healing. Some people see in these stories the influence of magic from the ancient work of Greece and Rome. They picture Jesus as a thaumaturge, invested with mysterious powers over the world of nature. If this interpretation is correct, we would have to say that Jesus' Jewish opponents were also correct in accusing Jesus of being a practitioner of the occult. But the Old Testament provides us with a different frame of reference for interpreting these stories. We have referred just now to the speech-acts of Jesus. They are like the speech-acts of God. In a speech-act the word that is uttered brings about the thing that is spoken about. Creation is brought into being by the word of God (Genesis 1:3, 6, 9, etc.; cf. Psalms 33:6, 9; 147:18). The words of Jesus follow the same pattern. They bring about that of which they speak.

The actions Mark proceeds to describe are small-scale acts focusing on Jesus. But they are comparable to God's large-scale acts generally. Mark's story of the stilling of the storm (Mark 4:35-41) leads directly to the account of the exorcism of the Gerasene demoniac (Mark 5:1-20). The two incidents are a counterpart to the description of what God does in Psalm 65:7: "who dost still the roaring of the seas, the roaring of their waves, the tumult of the peoples." Yahweh is the one who makes the storm be still and brings those who sail to their desired haven (Psalm 107:23-30; cf. 89:9).

Mark 6:47-52 tells of Jesus walking on the sea. This passage has its counterpart in the Old Testament description of God trampling the sea (Job 9:9; Habakkuk 3:15). Other stories recall events associated with Moses and Elijah. They are told with a view to showing Jesus as one greater than Moses and Elijah, who are seen in a vision at Jesus' transfiguration (Mark 9:2-8). It follows Peter's confession of Jesus as the Christ (Mark 8:27-30). Jesus is identified as God's " 'beloved Son; listen to him.' "

The accounts of the feeding of the five thousand (Mark 6:32-44) and of the four thousand (Mark 8:1-10) recall the stories of the exodus wanderings and the provision of manna and quails. But they also point forward to the messianic banquet. They are not two versions of the same story. Rather, they are two accounts that symbolize the offering of salvation "to the Jew first, but also to the Greek" (Romans 1:16). For the first is set in Jewish territory and the second is set in the Hellenistic region of Decapolis.

Who is Jesus? The idea that Jesus might be Elijah (Mark 6:15; 8:28) may have been prompted by two things. On the one hand, the return of Elijah was expected in the end time (Mark 9:12-13). On the other hand, Jesus was doing what Elijah and Elisha had done. Both made a small amount of food go a long way in time of need and restored a child to life (1 Kings 17; 2 Kings 4). Jesus fed the multitudes and restored life to Jairus's daughter (Mark 5:21-43). Through Elijah's successor, Elisha, Naaman was healed of his leprosy (2 Kings 5). Such healings were very rare in the Old Testament. Jesus had already healed a leper (Mark 1:40-44).

At the climax of these stories Jesus is confessed as one greater than John the Baptist, Elijah, or any of the prophets. The coming Elijah was not Jesus but John. Peter confesses, " 'You are the Christ' " (Mark 8:29). Mark's stories present Jesus as one who has done what God himself is said to do in Psalm 107. He has delivered from hunger in the wilderness (Mark 6:30-44; 8:1-10, 14-21; cf. Psalm 107:4-9). He has delivered from darkness and bondage (Mark 5:1-20; 6:13; 7:24-30; cf. Psalm 107:10-16). He has delivered from sickness (Mark 5:21–6:5, 13, 53-56; 7:31-37; 8:22-26; cf. Psalm 107:17-22). He has delivered from peril at sea (Mark 4:35-41; 6:45-52; cf. Psalm 107:23-32).

Psalm 107:17 declares that "Some were sick through their sinful ways." In response to their cry the LORD "sent forth his word, and healed them, and delivered them from destruction." Mark's account of Jesus' dealing with the paralytic illustrates and embodies this action of God. The Psalmist gave the call "Let them thank the LORD for his steadfast love, for his wonderful works to the sons of men! And let them offer sacrifices of thanksgiving, and tell of his deeds in songs of joy!" (Psalm 107:21-22). Mark concludes his account of the healing of the paralytic with a comment that seems to echo this theme: "And he rose, and immediately took up the pallet and went out before them all; so that they were all amazed and glorified God, saying, 'We never saw anything like this!' " (Mark 2:12). Similar responses are found on other occasions (Mark 1:27, 45; 4:41; 5:20, 42; 7:37).

In the center of these stories of provision and rescue stands the story of the imprisonment and beheading of John the Baptist (Mark 6:14-29). It serves as a reminder that God does not always come to the immediate relief of his servants. The debate in Mark 7 concerning what defiles a person returns to the theme of defilement and washing. The Pharisees are concerned with the prescribed ritual cleansing, which includes the washing (Greek *baptismous*) of vessels (Mark 7:4). In popular belief the washing may have been thought of as a defense against evil spirits. But Jesus is concerned to deal with the defilement that comes from the heart (Mark 7:21-22). Once more Jesus is brought into head-on conflict with the Pharisees. They are the ones who have rejected the commandments of God and substituted for it their own tradition (Mark 7:9-13). With this incident we are reminded once more of the theme of cleansing and consecration contained in John the Baptist's prophecy that " 'He will baptize you with the Holy Spirit.' " We are reminded too of the deep-seated conviction of the Pharisees that Jesus was possessed by Satan and that his teaching and actions flagrantly set aside the word of God.

Jesus' messiahship has set him on a collision course with the religious hierarchy. Jesus' activity has by no means met with universal approval. His mother and brothers appear to have been fearful as to what Jesus was getting himself into (Mark 3:31-35). The Gerasenes begged Jesus to leave their neighborhood (Mark 5:17). When Jesus came to his own country, he could not do many mighty works, and he marveled because of their unbelief (Mark 6:5-6). But the opposition of the religious leaders was something else. Grounded as it was in their perception of Jesus as a blasphemous worker of signs and wonders who was leading the people astray, only one result could follow—his suffering and death. It follows as a direct consequence of his being the Christ, the Son of Man

(Mark 8:29-31; 9:31; 10:33-34). Peter's well-meaning attempt to divert Jesus from this path is rejected as Satanic (Mark 8:33).

The various incidents that are told in Mark 9 and 10 further illustrate the power and the reality of the Kingdom of God. They tell of life in the Kingdom, as Jesus cleanses men and women from evil and consecrates them. They also tell of the price that has to be paid both by the Son of Man and by his would-be followers in prayer, giving, self-denial, marriage relationships, possessions, and persecution. We must leave readers to follow through Mark's narrative for themselves. But two points call for attention. Both concern baptism.

The Final "Baptism." The first of these points concerns the dispute among the disciples about who was to be the greatest. It leads to the pronouncement that " 'whoever would be first among you must be slave of all. For the Son of man also came not to be served but to serve, and to give his life as a ransom for many' " (Mark 10:44-45). Apparently out of the blue Jesus speaks of the cup he must drink and the baptism with which he must be baptized (Mark 10:38-39). The theme of the cup looks forward to the Last Supper (Mark 14:23-25) and is mentioned again in the Garden of Gethsemane (Mark 14:36). But the theme of the cup also carries with it memories of the cup of wrath and judgment (Isaiah 51:17-22; Jeremiah 25:15; Ezekiel 23:31-33; Habakkuk 2:16). The cup Jesus will have to drink will be a cup of wrath and judgment. In the eyes of his enemies his death will be a judgment that is well deserved and that has come none too soon. But in reality it will be a means of atonement and redemption beyond their conception.

In the same way the baptism Jesus now speaks of will be in the eyes of his opponents the means of purging the evil out of the midst of the people. By removing the evildoer the nation would be clean once more. From the standpoint of Jesus' opponents his death will be a baptism, a cleansing, a reconsecration of the people. But in reality it will have a significance beyond their conception. For it will indeed be the means by which God's people are cleansed and consecrated, through Jesus' bearing the divine wrath on himself.

The other point that calls for attention is the event we know as the cleansing of the temple, when Jesus drove out those who bought and sold (Mark 11:15-18). Jesus' purpose was that the cleansed temple might fulfil the prophecy, " ' "My house shall be called a house of prayer for all the nations" ' " (Mark 11:17; cf. Isaiah 56:7). Jesus' action follows upon his entry into Jerusalem. The crowds had welcomed him as " 'he who comes in the name of the Lord' " (Mark 11:9). They saw his coming as part of a coup that would establish the kingdom of their father David. But Mark intends us to see the cleansing of the temple as the climactic act that fulfils John's prophecy that " 'He will baptize you with the Holy Spirit.' " For that reason the event could equally well be called the "baptism of the temple."

From time to time I have spoken about prophetic signs—signs performed by the prophet that illustrated and embodied his message. They were like acted parables that spoke volumes for those with eyes to see. In entering Jerusalem on a colt he was acting out a parable and staking his claim to be the king spoken of by the prophet Zechariah: "Rejoice greatly, O daughter of Zion! Shout aloud, O daughter of Jerusalem! Lo, your king comes to you; triumphant and victorious is he, humble and riding on an ass, on a colt the foal of an ass" (Zechariah 9:9). Mark is content to describe the event, but Matthew (21:5) and John (12:15) spell out the point. In cleansing the temple Jesus was fulfilling the prophecy of Malachi 3. John the Baptist had fulfilled the prophecy of the coming Elijah. Now the LORD was indeed suddenly coming to his temple. Like a refiner's fire he was seeking to purify the sons of Levi, so that the offering of Judah and Jerusalem would be pleasing to the LORD.

Once more the question of Jesus' authority is raised (Mark 11:27-33). The chief priests, the scribes, and the elders ask Jesus, " 'By what authority are you doing these things, or who gave you this authority to do them?' " Perhaps they thought that Jesus was a self-styled messiah taking the law into his own hands. Perhaps they saw his act as a crazed piece of desecration. Perhaps they wondered whether he saw himself as a divinely inspired exorcist. Perhaps they wondered whether they had been right all along and that he was indeed possessed by Satan. At first sight Jesus' answer may seem to be evasive. The question belongs to a whole series of dilemmas that surface in the final days of Jesus' ministry. Should Jews pay taxes to Caesar (Mark 12:13-17)? What about marriage relationships in the resurrection (Mark 12:18-27)? What is the great commandment (Mark 12:28-35)? These questions that were put to Jesus were designed to test his orthodoxy, to see whether he was a true teacher or one who was leading people astray, and to trip him up. Jesus' replies and his counterquestion—How can the Christ be the Son of David if David himself, inspired by the Spirit, calls him Lord? (Mark 12:35-37)—point his questioners to the ways of God and raise the question of his own identity. In none of his answers did Jesus evade the issue, not least in reply to the question of his authority to cleanse the temple.

Jesus' counterquestion forces his interrogators to think through their position. " 'Was the baptism of John from heaven [i.e., from God] or from men? Answer me.' " The questioners follow through the logic of the question, but in the end decline to give an answer. Because they will not face up to the logic of the situation, Jesus also refuses to give a point-blank answer. The questioners were afraid to say that John's authority derived from men because they feared the people, "for all held that John was a real prophet." Perhaps, too, they shared that belief in their hearts, though evidently they had not declared their support of John or protested against his imprisonment and execution. But they also saw full well what Jesus' next question would be, if they were to admit that John the Baptist had received his authority from God. It would simply be: " ' "Why then did you not believe him?" ' "

The question of John's authority was directly related to Jesus' authority. It was John who had baptized Jesus, and it was after Jesus' baptism by John that the Spirit came upon Jesus to anoint him as the messianic Son. Moreover, John had said, " 'I have baptized you with water; but he will baptize you with the Holy Spirit.' " This was the answer to the question of the interrogators. What Jesus had done had been done in the power and authority of the Spirit, as the Spirit-anointed Christ. His action in cleansing the temple was the climactic fulfilment of John's prophecy that " 'he will baptize you with the Holy Spirit.' "

Jesus' act of cursing the fig tree (Mark 11:12-14, 20-21) is an acted parable of judgment on failure to respond. The parable of the vineyard (Mark 12:1-12) is a commentary on what is happening. Despite the acclaim of the crowds on the first Palm Sunday, there is little positive response to Jesus. The only bright spots on the darkening scene are the widow who gave her all in the service of God (Mark 12:41-44) and the woman who anointed Jesus in the house of Simon the leper (Mark 14:3-9). At the beginning and close of Jesus' ministry there is an act of anointing. He was anointed by the Spirit at the beginning. Now at the end Jesus says that the woman " 'has done what she could; she has anointed my body beforehand for burying.' "

The discourse in Mark 13 warns of the impending destruction of the temple and the coming tribulation. The disciples of Jesus will be beaten in synagogues. They will stand before governors and kings for Jesus' sake, to bear testimony to them. But the gospel must be preached to all nations. In time of trial the Holy Spirit will tell the disciples what to say (Mark 13:11). In words that echo Deuteronomy 13 and the motives underlying the charge against Jesus, Jesus warns against those who will *lead astray* (Mark 13:5-6). " 'False Christs and false prophets will arise and show signs and wonders to lead astray, if possible, the elect' " (Mark 13:23). But the disciples are not to lose heart or be led astray. Although no one—not even the Son—knows the hour (Mark 13:32), the Son will be vindicated and will fulfil the prophecy of Daniel 7:13. " 'And then they will see the Son of man coming in clouds with great power and glory. And he will send out the angels, and gather his elect from the four winds, from the ends of the earth to the ends of heaven' " (Mark 13:26-27). In the meantime, the disciples are to " 'Watch' " (Mark 13:36).

Mark's narrative leads on to the account of Judas's betrayal, the Last Supper, Jesus' agony in Gethsemane, his arrest, trial, crucifixion, and burial (Mark 14:10–15:47). The high priest secures from Jesus the admission that he is " 'the Christ, the Son of the Blessed,' " which he immediately denounces as blasphemy. The Sanhedrin agrees that it is blasphemy worthy of death. To Pilate all this translates as meaning that Jesus is " 'The King of the Jews.' " He consents to this charge, and an inscription is made of it. The scoffers invite Jesus to prophesy and perform a miracle to save himself, a hint that Jesus was still perceived as a wonder-working false prophet. But no prophecy or saving miracle is forthcoming. Jesus dies in pain, weakness, and desolation. The centurion who saw him die gives his verdict, " 'Truly this man was the Son of God' " (Mark 15:39).

With this verdict we are reminded of the opening words of Mark. Mark brings his account to a close with a brief description of the burial of Jesus and the discovery of the empty tomb. The disciples are told by a young man in a white robe that Jesus has risen. The disciples are to go to Galilee, where they will see him. The Gospel closes on a note of fear and astonishment. (The longer and shorter endings that are printed in some Bibles are later additions to the original Gospel of Mark.) "And they went out and fled from the tomb; for trembling and astonishment had come upon them; and they said nothing to anyone, for they were afraid."

10/Remaking the Puzzle

Step 2: The Pictures of Matthew, Luke, and John

> *And there was much muttering about him among the people. While some said, "He is a good man," others said, "No, he is leading the people astray."* (John 7:12)

> *The Jews answered him, "Are we not right in saying that you are a Samaritan and have a demon?"* (John 8:48)

> *So the chief priests and the Pharisees gathered the council, and said, "What are we to do? For this man performs many signs. If we let him go on thus, every one will believe in him, and the Romans will come and destroy both our holy place and our nation."* (John 11:47-48)

It is now time to turn to the other three accounts of Jesus. Matthew and Luke follow the same basic outline as Mark. John gives an independent perspective. It would take too long to go through each of the three remaining Gospels point by point. Instead, I want to focus on the way they saw the miracles fitting into the total picture.

In looking at Mark we noted two neglected factors in reading the Gospel: the prophecy of John the Baptist that " 'He will baptize you with the Holy Spirit,' " and the directions in Deuteronomy 13 on what to do with workers of signs and wonders who lead the people astray. These two factors are keys to understanding what is going on not only in Mark but also in Matthew, Luke, and John.

THE GOSPEL ACCORDING TO MATTHEW

Features of Matthew. Matthew was written for Jewish readers. He records teaching like the Sermon on the Mount (Matthew 5–7) that spells out how Jesus stood in relation to the law and the prophets. He came not to destroy, but to fulfil them; not the smallest letter shall pass from the law until it has been fulfilled (Matthew 5:17-20). Matthew is deeply aware of the Jewish opposition to Jesus and also of the worldwide mission to non-Jews (Matthew 28:18-20). With this in mind Matthew follows the same basic outline of Jesus' life, ministry, death, and resurrection. But he fills out many things that Mark gives only in the barest outline. Both Matthew and Luke include teaching that is not given by Mark.

All four Gospels tell us about the ministry and message of John the Baptist. All four tell of Jesus' relationship to John and spotlight John's identification of Jesus as the one whose ministry it is to baptize with the Holy Spirit (Matthew 3:11; Mark 1:8; Luke 3:16; John 1:33). But Matthew and Luke also give accounts of Jesus' conception and birth. Both of them attribute the conception of Jesus to the Holy Spirit (Matthew 1:18, 20; Luke 1:35). It is as if they both wish to counter any suggestion of adoptionism—that Jesus started off as a human being but was later endowed with divinity through his reception of the Spirit at his baptism (Matthew 3:16; Luke 3:22). They are saying in effect: Jesus was conceived by the Spirit, but he entered his messianic office as the Christ when the Spirit descended upon him after his baptism.

Two Phases. In Matthew, as in Mark and Luke, there are really two main phases in Jesus' ministry. The first phase is the period that begins with his return from the temptations in the wilderness and that continues to his cleansing of the temple. It is a period in which Jesus performs mighty acts of God. The second phase is confined to the final days of Jesus' ministry in which no miracles are performed at all. It is a period of weakness; it is the period of the passion. It is also the period of the triumph of the cross.

In the first of these two periods that Matthew describes, the presence of God is experienced through Jesus. He is active in strength. Jesus is the healer of Israel (Matthew 8:16-17; cf. Isaiah 53:4; Matthew 9:33). His ministry is directed not toward the disciples, but toward the crowds, the sick, the outsiders. Jesus' power and the faith of men and women is the recurring theme in the healing miracles of this phase of Jesus' ministry. But the nature miracles are rare. The lessons to be learned from them are lessons for the disciples (Matthew 8:23-27; 14:13-33; 15:29-39; 17:24-27; 21:18-22). The disciples themselves are given authority to participate in the work of Jesus (Matthew 10:1, 8).

The Message of the Miracles. As in the other Gospels, the miracles are like parables. Discernment of their meaning requires faith, a right attitude, and grace. This is true of the parables (Matthew 13:10-17; cf. Mark 4:11; Luke 8:9-10) as well as of the miracles. In response to the message sent by John the Baptist from prison as to whether he really is the Christ, Jesus points to his healing and preaching work in terms that recall the prophecies of Isaiah 29:18-19; 35:5-6 and 61:1. But Jesus adds, " 'And blessed is he who takes no offense at me' " (Matthew 11:6; cf. Luke 7:23). The healing miracles and the teaching of Jesus are characterized by the fact that they fulfil messianic prophecy. This is what distinguishes Jesus from other wonder workers and teachers.

Although Jesus healed many, he did not perform miracles for everyone. He did not perform one for John—even though the liberation of the imprisoned belongs to the messianic prophecy of Isaiah 61:1. This could well have caused offense. For John stood in a special relationship to him, while others who were healed were total strangers. How many of them went on to become disciples? Not to receive a miracle and still have faith is a blessing indeed! To see Jesus' messianic work for others while still suffering oneself, and yet not to be offended—this is true blessing!

Recognition of Jesus as the Christ, the Son of the living God, is itself a gift that comes from God (Matthew 16:17; cf. 11:27). People generally thought that Jesus was a prophet—perhaps even the reincarnation of John the Baptist, Elijah, or Jeremiah. Evidently they took his works to be prophetic signs. But Peter discerned that Jesus was more than a prophet. He was the Lord's anointed, the Christ.

Matthew's version of Peter's confession is slightly different from that of Mark and Luke. Mark gives it as " 'You are the Christ' " (Mark 8:29). Luke has " 'The Christ of God' " (Luke 9:20). Matthew has " 'You are the Christ, the Son of the living God' " (Matthew 16:17). But this is not, as some critics suggest, a heightened Christology that goes beyond Mark and Luke. It is not as if Peter is on a quiz show, and having given the right answer to the first question, he goes on for the jackpot. The confession takes the form of a Hebrew parallelism in which the second phrase repeats in different words what is said in the first phrase. In view of what we said in Chapter 8 about the titles of Jesus, "Son of God" is here a title of messianic kingship. To confess Jesus as the Christ is to confess him as the messianic king. It is also to confess him as the one anointed by the Spirit. It is to see the teaching and the miracles of Jesus as the teaching and the miracles of the Lord's anointed.

Matthew makes it crystal clear that not all miracles come from God. The Sermon on the Mount recognizes the possibility of prophesying, casting out demons, and doing many mighty works in Jesus' name, only to be cast out as an evildoer not known by Jesus (Matthew 7:21-23). In warning the disciples of the impending judgment and tribulation, Jesus gives warning of false Christs in terms reminiscent of Deuteronomy 13: " 'For false Christs and false prophets will arise and show great signs and wonders, so as to lead astray, if possible, even the elect' " (Matthew 24:24). This warning echoes the thought that underlies the charges against Jesus himself.

The Beelzebul Charge and the Sign of Jonah. The charge that Jesus is possessed by Beelzebul occupies a central place in Matthew (12:24). But the whole episode is given with much greater detail than in Mark. Once more the issue is whether Jesus is possessed by Satan or whether the Holy Spirit has been put upon him. Matthew gives the same basic facts of the charge and Jesus' reply that Mark gives. But he also gives certain significant additions. He points out that Jesus healed all who followed him (Matthew 12:15). He adds that

> This was to fulfil what was spoken by the prophet Isaiah: "Behold, my servant whom I have chosen, my beloved with whom my soul is well pleased. I will put my Spirit upon him, and he shall proclaim justice to the Gentiles. He will not wrangle or cry aloud, nor will any one hear his voice in the streets; he will not break a bruised reed or quench a smoldering wick, till he brings justice to victory; and in his name will the Gentiles hope." (Matthew 12:17-21; cf. Isaiah 42:1-4)

This passage was quoted earlier by the "voice from heaven" after Jesus' baptism and the descent of the Spirit upon him like a dove (Matthew 3:17). It draws attention to three things: the role of the Spirit in Jesus' work, the gentle, righteous character of that work, and its significance for the world at large beyond Judaism.

Like Mark, Matthew shows how Jesus demolished the charge of casting out demons by Beelzebul by showing that it contradicts itself. Like Mark, Matthew records Jesus' pronouncement on blasphemy against the Holy Spirit. In the context of the immediate events and of the Gospel at large the unforgivable sin is the blasphemous attribution to Satan of what is in fact the work of the Holy Spirit.

Following a series of sayings on the way people speak,

Matthew reports an incident that receives only passing notice in Mark. Some of the scribes and Pharisees say to Jesus, " 'Teacher, we wish to see a sign from you' " (Matthew 12:38; cf. Mark 8:11; Luke 11:16, 29). This leads to the saying about the sign of Jonah that is also given by Luke and that is mentioned again in Matthew 16:4.

Some scholars think that the saying about the sign of Jonah is an invention of the early church, designed to justify its faith in the resurrection. At all events, the request for a sign is generally interpreted as a request by a group of "Don't-Knows" who would like a bit of extra evidence to help them make up their minds about Jesus. Just one more sign will clinch it for them. But Jesus refuses. He does not do signs on demand. If people cannot make up their minds by now, he is not going to pander to them by doing a miracle just for show.

I think that this last point is true enough. The miracles of Jesus were not designed simply to impress. They were done for their own sake. Jesus was not interested in a type of "power evangelism" that drew people in by impressive spectacles. If he had been, he would have listened to Satan's invitation and jumped off the temple, or made a deal with him to get the following of all the kingdoms of the world (Matthew 4:1-11). But there is more to it than this.

The incident follows the Beelzebul charge—that Jesus is in league with Satan. Such a league is exactly what Satan proposed in the temptation of Jesus. But Jesus rejected such a deal, and he throws out the charge. It is patently absurd. But Jesus' opponents are now regrouping themselves. They try a new tack. If only Jesus will perform a sign before them— then they will have him trapped! The inquirers have nothing to lose. If by chance Jesus were to speak something in the name of the Lord that came to pass, he might conceivably be regarded as a prophet or even the eschatological prophet. But if he performed a feat of magic, the previous suspicions would be confirmed and he would be put to death (cf. Deuteronomy 18:9-22).

In Mark the request comes after the feeding of the four thousand. If only Jesus will repeat a miracle like that, they will have clear-cut evidence that he is indeed a magician, a worker of signs and wonders, who is performing such feats in order to lead the people astray. It will be a sign, moreover, that does not depend on hearsay. It will have been done before competent witnesses, namely, themselves.

Jesus replies by referring to the sign of Jonah (Matthew 12:40; 16:4; cf. Luke 11:29-30). We have already talked about prophetic signs. They were done by the prophet to illustrate and embody his message. But the sign of Jonah is different. It is not a sign done by the prophet; it is a sign done *to* the prophet.

The Book of Jonah tells how Jonah was commanded to go to Nineveh, but instead took a ship to Tarshish. A storm came up, and the crew realized that an evildoer was on board. There is nothing for them to do but to throw the evildoer overboard and remove the offense that was causing the storm. And so the storm abates. But Jonah is rescued by the great fish. After three days and three nights in the belly of the fish he is restored.

In effect, Jesus is saying that the Jewish leaders will treat him in the same way the crew of the ship treated Jonah. They see him as an evildoer who must be gotten rid of in order to save the ship of state. Like the crew they think they are acting in righteousness. But as God came to Jonah's rescue, he will ultimately come to the rescue of Jesus and restore him.

The sign is not one that Jesus will perform in order to oblige those who requested it. It is they who will take the initiative. But it is the Father who will ultimately give the sign in raising Jesus from the dead. The sign of Jonah has further ramifications, which could be seen by those familiar with the Book of Jonah and the Hebrew language. As we stressed earlier, faith and discernment are needed in order to understand.

In the story of Jonah both the crew and Jonah see the need to avert divine wrath by sacrificing Jonah. Similarly in the history of Jesus both Jesus' enemies and Jesus himself saw his death as a means of atonement—but for different reasons. Jesus' enemies saw his death as a means of purging the evil out of the midst of the people. Thus a national disaster would be averted. But Jesus saw his death as the means of making atonement (Matthew 20:28; 26:28).

A further ramification is the meaning of the name "Jonah." "Jonah" means "dove." When Jesus talked about the sign of the prophet Jonah, his words could be translated as the sign of the prophet "Dove." They recall the descent of the Spirit "like a dove" after his baptism. For those who discern it the name carries with it an allusion to the Spirit. Moreover, it was precisely on account of the Spirit's activity through Jesus that he was being accused of being possessed by Satan. As we have seen, Jesus had already rebutted the charge as self-contradictory and absurd. But Matthew records a saying that links the work of the Spirit through Jesus with the presence of the Kingdom of God: " 'But if it is by the Spirit that I cast out demons, then the kingdom of God has come upon you' " (Matthew 12:28).

All this sheds light on the way Jesus addressed Simon Peter as Simon Bar-Jona (i.e., Simon son of Jonah) in Matthew 16:17. Simon was his original name. He had confessed Jesus as the Christ, the Son of the living God. Jesus replies: " 'Blessed are you, Simon Bar-Jona! For flesh and blood has not revealed this to you, but my Father who is in heaven.' " It does not mean that Simon's father was called Jonah. It means that Simon has come into a new relationship with Jesus. (See Matthew 9:2 for another case of Jesus addressing someone as his son.) The Old Testament speaks of the sons of the prophets. Simon had become, as it were, a son of the new Jonah. It is as if he had been born again! At this point he receives a new name, Peter (i.e., Rock), and is given a unique place in the founding of the church.

The Paradox of Power and Weakness. At the outset of this brief account of Matthew's perspective I suggested that there were two main phases in Jesus' ministry. The first is marked by Jesus' mighty works of power. It extends to his entry into Jerusalem on the first Palm Sunday. The second is marked by an absence of such mighty works. It is the final week of Jesus' ministry. It is a time of teaching but not of miracles. It culminates in his death on the cross, when he let go the spirit (Matthew 27:50)—perhaps an allusion to both the human spirit and the Holy Spirit (cf. Psalm 51).

The distinction between two successive phases in Jesus' life is not, however, an absolute one. In the earlier phase there was weakness as well as power. He who stilled the storm had nowhere to lay his head (Matthew 8:20-27). Sheer fatigue caused him to sleep in the boat. He who cast out demons into the herd of swine obliged the Gadarenes by leaving their neighborhood (Matthew 8:34).

A paradox of power and weakness runs straight through Matthew's story. Jesus fulfilled the Emmanuel prophecy of Isaiah (Matthew 1:23; cf. Isaiah 7:14). But the circumstances of his birth were humble in the extreme. As an infant he received royal gifts from the Magi, but when Mary was first found to be pregnant, Joseph's first thought was that the child was illegitimate (Matthew 1:19; cf. 2:11). As Son of God Jesus has dominion and authority (Matthew 11:27; 14:30, 33; 16:16; 22:42-44; 28:19). But the way of the Son of God is that of righteous obedience and self-denial in the face of temptation (Matthew 3:15; 4:3-10).

The paradox of power and weakness comes to a climax in the trial and death of Jesus. The chief priests, scribes, and elders mock him, saying: " 'He saved others; he cannot save himself. He is the King of Israel; let him come down now from the cross, and we will believe in him. He trusts in God; let God deliver him now, if he desires him; for he said, "I am the Son of God" ' " (Matthew 27:42-43). The situation has a striking parallel in the Wisdom of Solomon 2:18: "For if the righteous man is God's son, he will uphold him and deliver him out of the hand of his adversaries."

But no such deliverance comes to Jesus. He declines to prophesy (Matthew 26:68). There is no miraculous rescue from the cross (Matthew 27:45-50). The theme of Jesus' kingship is very prominent in the account of his trial and execution (Matthew 27:11, 29, 37, 40, 42). It is taken by Jesus' opponents to be an absurd claim that has finally been rendered baseless. But the title "King of Israel" was one that belonged to Yahweh (e.g., Isaiah 44:6). In an ultimate act of irony, what the enemies of Jesus are doing they are doing to God himself through his anointed Son.

Much has been written about Jesus' cry from the cross, " 'Eli, Eli, lama sabach-thani' "—" 'My God, my God, why hast thou forsaken me?' " (Matthew 27:46; cf. Mark 15:34). To some of the bystanders it sounded like a cry to Elijah. From the perspective of magic, necromancy, and occultism this would have sounded like a last desperate effort to invoke supernatural power. The words themselves express utter desolation. They are also the opening words of Psalm 22. All four evangelists see aspects of this Psalm fulfilled in the passion of Jesus (Psalm 22:7-8; cf. Matthew 27:39, 43; Mark 15:29; Luke 23:35; Psalm 22:18; cf. Matthew 27:35; Mark 15:24; Luke 23:34; John 19:24). But Matthew goes further. The final verses of the Psalm find a fulfilment in the final verses of Matthew's Gospel. The universal dominion that belongs to the LORD in the Psalm (verses 27-31) is given to the risen Lord (Matthew 28:18).

THE GOSPEL ACCORDING TO LUKE

Features of Luke. Luke follows the same basic outline that we have found in Matthew and Mark. But he omits some of Mark's stories and adds some of his own. He does not tell us about Jesus walking on the water, the Syrophoenician woman's daughter, the deaf-mute, the feeding of the four thousand, the blind man at Bethsaida, or the cursing of the fig tree. But he includes the catch of fish (Luke 5:1-11), the healing of the centurion's servant (Luke 7:1-10), the raising of the widow of Nain's son (Luke 7:11-17), the healing of the ten lepers (Luke 17:11-19), and the story of the high priest's servant's ear (Luke 22:50-51). Luke also includes teaching that the others do not have. If it were not for Luke, we would not know the parables of the Good Samaritan (Luke 10:30-37), the lost sheep, the lost coin, and the lost son (Luke 15:3-32).

In telling his stories Luke strives for precision. He directs attention away from the recipient toward Jesus himself. He notes the crowd's reaction. He brings out the importance of the miracles for Jesus' mission and their significance for discipleship. Luke brings out the relationship between Jesus' miracles and his teaching. Even more than Mark, Luke stresses the role of the Spirit.

Luke's View of the Spirit. Not only does Luke stress the role of the Spirit in the conception of Jesus (Luke 1:35), the expectation of his coming (Luke 1:67; 2:26-27), and Jesus' baptism (Luke 3:16, 22), but he also points out that Jesus, "full of the Holy Spirit, returned from the Jordan, and was led by the Spirit" in his wilderness temptations (Luke 4:1). He then "returned in the power of the Spirit into Galilee" (Luke 4:14). Luke describes an event at the beginning of Jesus' ministry that the other Gospels do not. He has already visited other synagogues. But now Jesus enters the synagogue at Nazareth where he was brought up. As was his custom, he goes to the synagogue on the sabbath day. Standing up to read, he is given the book of the prophet Isaiah. He finds the place where it is written:

> "The Spirit of the Lord is upon me, because he has anointed me to preach good news to the poor. He has sent me to proclaim release to the captives and recovering of sight to the blind, to set at liberty those who are oppressed, to proclaim the acceptable year of the Lord." (Luke 4:18-19; cf. Isaiah 61:1-2)

Whereupon Jesus closes the book and gives it back to the attendant. He sits down and declares, " 'Today this scripture has been fulfilled in your hearing.' "

In recording this incident, Luke is telling us that Jesus is to be understood in the light of this prophecy concerning the Spirit. It underlines and complements what John the Baptist has said about Jesus and the Spirit (Luke 3:16) and what the "voice from heaven" has said (Luke 3:22). It represents Jesus' own understanding of himself and his mission. It stresses teaching, healing, and release. It fulfils in greater measure what the Year of Jubilee represented in the Old Testament (cf. Exodus 21:2-6; Leviticus 25:1-55; Deuteronomy 15:12-18).

Audience Reaction. Although people wonder at his gracious words, their attitude turns quickly to one of hostility—especially when Jesus reminds them that there were many widows in the time of Elijah, but Elijah was sent to only one, a foreigner, and there were many lepers in Israel in the time of Elisha, but only Naaman, a Syrian, was cleansed. The people are so aroused that they attempt to kill Jesus by throwing him over a cliff. But he passes through them and goes his way (Luke 4:30).

Luke often draws attention to people's response to Jesus. Frequently it is a combination of amazement, fear, and glorification (Luke 5:25-26; 7:16; 8:35, 37, 47; 9:43; 13:13; 17:15; 18:43), though fear is generally confined to the onlookers. If faith is a ground of healing, praise to God is the proper response (Luke 17:18-19). Mighty works—whether performed by Jesus or by his disciples—show that the Kingdom of God is present. It demands a response (Luke 10:9, 13-20; 11:14-23; 17:20-21). The Kingdom of God is not something in the future. It is already here through Jesus and the Spirit.

Conflict with Satan. Like Matthew and Mark, Luke brings out the conflict with Satan and the question whether it is by the Spirit of God or Beelzebul that Jesus does his works. But Luke mentions things that are not in the other Gospels. Jesus sends out seventy disciples in advance of his own coming. The subjection of the demons to them is a sign of the downfall of Satan (Luke 10:17-20). The return of the seventy is an occasion for Jesus' own rejoicing in the Spirit (Luke 10:21). Luke places the saying about blasphemy against the Holy Spirit in the context of a series of sayings (Luke 12:10) and thus detaches it from the Beelzebul controversy (Luke 11:14-26). Nevertheless, the controversy occupies a pivotal place.

Sickness. One of the things that Luke does is to bring out connections. He sees connections between illness and the powers of evil. The Beelzebul charge is prompted by the casting out of "a demon that was dumb" (Luke 11:14). It leads to the comment, " 'But if it is by the finger of God that I cast out demons, then the kingdom of God has come upon you' " (Luke 11:20). Here the expression "finger of God" is used (like the more common "hand of God") as a way of speaking about the Spirit of God. The healing of a woman who had "a spirit of infirmity" for eighteen years is described as a release from the bondage of Satan (Luke 13:10, 16; cf. 11:21-22). In his account of the healing of Simon Peter's mother-in-law, Luke uses the language of exorcism. He tells how Jesus "rebuked the fever" (Luke 4:39). In describing his mission, Jesus closely links the casting out of demons, healing, and prophecy (Luke 13:31-35).

The Spirit and the Disciples. But Luke also stresses another connection—the connection between the Spirit and the disciples. If Jesus is anointed by the Spirit and works in the power of the Spirit, the disciples are also promised the Spirit. In the Sermon on the Mount Matthew records a saying about the Father's delight to " 'give things to those who ask him' " (Matthew 7:11). Luke spells out the nature of these gifts. They are the gifts of the Holy Spirit to those who ask the Father (Luke 11:13). When Luke gives his version of the saying about blasphemy against the Holy Spirit, he goes on to link it with the promise that the Holy Spirit will teach the disciples what to say in their hour of trial (Luke 12:12; cf. Matthew 10:20).

These sayings form a bridge between Luke and the Book of Acts. For Luke and Acts form a two-volume work that presents an account of Christianity from its beginning to the time of Paul's imprisonment in Rome. Together they are a defense of Christianity written at a time when the church was growing vigorously, but when it was also under attack. The opening words of the Gospel of Luke and of the Acts of the Apostles have a common theme (Luke 1:1-4; Acts 1:1-5). Luke tells of Jesus and his ministry as the Christ, anointed by the Spirit, which culminates with his resurrection and ascension (Luke 24). Acts begins with ascension and Pentecost (Acts 1 and 2) and tells of the continued work of Christ through the Spirit in the church.

THE GOSPEL ACCORDING TO JOHN

In different ways Matthew, Mark, and Luke stress the role of the Spirit in their Christology. They have an explicit Spirit Christology. At the same time they have what might be called an implicit Word Christology. With John it is the other way around. He begins with an explicit Word Christology. But this also leads to an implicit Spirit Christology.

John's "Word Christology." John begins his Gospel with words that recall the account of creation in Genesis 1.

> In the beginning was the Word, and the Word was with God, and the Word was God. He was in the beginning with God; all things were made through him, and without him was not anything made that was made. (John 1:1-3)

John goes on to say: "And the Word became flesh and dwelt among us, full of grace and truth; we have beheld his glory,

glory as of the only Son from the Father" (John 1:14).

It is as if John is telling us: If we want to understand Jesus in the widest possible context, we must realize that the works of Jesus were none other than the works of him who is the agent of all creation. The divine agent who made all things is the one who was present and active in the human life of Jesus. The same creative Word of the Father that created all things is the creative and redemptive Word that was at work in the works of Jesus. When John speaks of the "Son," he means the eternal Word of the Father who became incarnate in Jesus. As such, he is divine. He existed before all things. He is the Father's executor in all things (John 1:3, 9; 3:16-21, 31-36; 6:33, 50, 58, 63; 7:28; 8:14-20; 10:36; 16:28; 17:1-5, 17, 21-24).

John's "Spirit Christology." John begins with an explicit Word Christology. But his Gospel culminates in an explicit Spirit Christology. The risen Jesus breathes on the disciples and says to them, " 'Receive the Holy Spirit' " (John 20:22). To Western readers this episode sounds odd. It is difficult to envisage. But once again we have a prophetic sign. In both Greek and Hebrew the word "spirit" means "wind" and "breath." Breath is a symbol of life. No human being can live without it. Jesus lived not only by human breath, but by the divine breath, the Spirit. And in this prophetic sign, Jesus bestows on the disciples the divine breath that was his.

Between the opening words of the prologue and this act of bestowing the Spirit John sets forth his account of Jesus' ministry. As he does so, the theme of the Spirit unfolds. The ministry of John the Baptist is described. "And John bore witness, 'I saw the Spirit descend as a dove from heaven, and it remained on him. I myself did not know him; but he who sent me to baptize with water said to me, "He on whom you see the Spirit descend and remain, this is he who baptizes with the Holy Spirit" ' " (John 1:32-33).

The Spirit figures prominently in the discussion with Nicodemus. Unless one is born of water and the Spirit, one cannot enter the Kingdom of God (John 3:5). Jesus tells the Samaritan woman that the hour is coming, and now is, when true worshipers will worship the Father in spirit and in truth (John 4:23). The Paraclete sayings of John 14:16-17, 25 and 16:7-15 form a bridge between Jesus' possession of the Spirit and his bestowal of the Spirit. The world cannot receive the Spirit, but the disciples are reminded that " 'You know him for he dwells with you, and will be in you' " (John 14:17). However, the Spirit is not given to believers as an inner source of living water until Jesus is glorified (John 7:39).

Charges against Jesus. Matthew, Mark, and Luke give prominence to the Beelzebul charge. John records the equally damning charge that Jesus is a Samaritan and has a demon (John 8:48; cf. 7:20; 10:20). Here again the charge is linked with attempts to kill Jesus on the grounds that he is leading the people astray (John 7:12, 20, 25; 8:59; 10:33). Maybe they saw Jesus' teaching as a form of Samaritan deviation from the pure Jewish faith. Maybe the fact that Jesus spent time in Samaria and actually mixed with the Samaritans was enough to brand him as a Samaritan.

To our ears the term "Samaritan" suggests compassion, caring, and what is best in people. But this is because of Jesus' parable of the Good Samaritan in Luke 10. To Jewish ears in the first century "Samaritan" had other associations. It meant someone who belonged to a people who had corrupted the pure religion of the Scriptures. It meant someone who rejected the divinely appointed worship in the temple at Jerusalem in favor of another brand of religion on Mount Gerizim. This religion was basically pagan, with a thin veneer of Old Testament religion. To the orthodox Jew, Samaritanism was hardly better than the heathen religion of the Gentiles. Added to all this are hints of belief in magic and the demonic

(John 4:11; Acts 8:9-24). To those who did not take the trouble to look too deeply into it, the charge that Jesus was a Samaritan who had a demon was plausible enough to make it stick. Perhaps the Samaritans' reception of Jesus as the Christ (John 4:25-42) contributed to his rejection by the Jewish leaders.

The high priest Caiaphas justified the death of Jesus as an act of expediency that would avert the national disaster that would come about through the people being led astray by Jesus' signs (John 11:47-53). With this we are brought back once more to the same basic charge against Jesus that runs through all four Gospels. He is not simply an unorthodox teacher. He is a worker of signs and wonders who uses these acts to bolster his false teaching that leads the people astray. The teacher, the teaching, and all his works are seen as diabolical.

The charge of blasphemy figures in John 10:33, 36. It is linked with Jesus' claim to be the Son of God. It is answered with the reply: " 'If I am not doing the works of my Father, then do not believe me; but if I do them, even though you do not believe me, believe the works, that you may know and understand that the Father is in me and I am in the Father' " (John 10:37-38).

The Works of the Father. The other Gospel writers develop the thought that the works of Jesus are the works of the Spirit-anointed Christ. As such, he is the expected Son of God who fulfils messianic prophecy. John develops the theme that the works of Jesus can be recognized as the works of the Father. In reply to Philip's request to be shown the Father, Jesus asks:

> "Do you not believe that I am in the Father and the Father in me? The words that I say to you I do not speak on my own authority; but the Father who dwells in me does his works. Believe me that I am in the Father and the Father in me; or else believe me for the sake of the works themselves." (John 14:10-11)

Other passages that develop this theme are John 5:20-27, 35-40; 7:27-28; 8:28; 9:3-4; 15:24; 17:2-4, 21. Jesus' works are identifiable as the works of the Father. As such they reveal the divine glory, and they bring glory to God (John 5:41-47; cf. 1:14; 2:11; 7:18; 8:50, 54; 9:24; 11:4, 40; 12:41, 43; 17:5, 22, 24). It is a mark of human beings—especially the accusers of Jesus—that they seek their own glory. It is the mark of Jesus' works that they manifest the glory of God and bring glory to God.

Miracles as Signs. In John the miracles of Jesus are called *works* and *signs.* As such, they are not *proofs* that are external to the message. They do not stand outside the message as guarantees of the truth of the message, like the sign requested in John 6:30. They are part of the revelation itself. They are like the prophetic signs in the Old Testament that illustrated and embodied the message. Most prophetic signs in the Old Testament were nonsupernatural. They did not involve any violation of the laws of nature. They were drawn from everyday life. It was their meaning that pointed beyond nature.

Jesus too performed such prophetic signs. He rode into Jerusalem on an ass, acting out the prophecy of Zechariah (John 12:15; Zechariah 9:9). He washed the disciples' feet (John 13:12-27). But his miracles also had the character of prophetic signs. The feeding of the five thousand provokes the comment, " 'This is indeed the prophet who is to come into the world!' " (John 6:14). The comment recalls the expectation of the great prophet of the end time (Deuteronomy 18:15-19; cf. Acts 3:22-23; 7:37). But insofar as Jesus was more than a prophet—in fact, the Word of God made flesh— his signs also have a supernatural character.

In Matthew, Mark, and Luke, the casting out of demons plays a big part in Jesus' ministry. John makes no mention of particular exorcisms, but he reports Jesus' saying about the judgment of this world and the casting out of its ruler

(John 12:31). This is the ultimate exorcism. It comes about through Jesus' death.

John alludes to many signs and works that Jesus did, but he picks out seven to describe in detail: the turning of water into wine (John 2:1-11); the healing of the nobleman's son (John 4:46-54); the healing of the lame man by the pool (John 5:1-18); the feeding of the five thousand (John 6:1-14); the walking on the water (John 6:16-21); the healing of the blind man (John 9:1-41); and the raising of Lazarus (John 11:1-44). Some of these are mentioned or at least have parallels in the other Gospels, but others are not. The raising of Lazarus prompts the Jewish leaders to act against Jesus and liquidate him.

The choice of the seven signs may reflect the idea of the perfect number, completeness, the days of creation, or the restoration of creation. The theme of the redemption and restoration of creation fits in with the opening words of John's Gospel, which recall the original creation in Genesis 1. The signs in John reveal Jesus' lordship over space, time, nature, disease, calamity, and death. John's story reaches its climax with the conclusion:

> Now Jesus did many other signs in the presence of the disciples, which are not written in this book; but these are written that you may believe that Jesus is the Christ, the Son of God, and that believing you may have life in his name. (John 20:30-31)

The signs of Jesus manifest who he is and also the Father through him. But the words and works of Jesus have a divisive effect on people. Jesus repeatedly provokes a double reaction (John 7:12, 40-41; 9:16; 10:19; 11:45-46). Jesus provokes belief (John 2:11, 23; 4:50, 53; 5:9; 6:14, 21; 9:11, 17, 33, 38; 11:27, 45; 12:11). But he also provokes unbelief (John 5:18; 6:66; 9:16, 24, 29, 40-41; 11:53) There are those who desire signs and wonders but who never get beyond that point (John 2:24-25; 3:2; 4:48; 6:2; 12:18). There are those who have seen and believe. But the truly blessed are those " 'who have not seen and yet believe' " (John 20:29).

Some books state their conclusions at the end. John states his at the beginning. The eternal Word of God, the Creator, took flesh and became a human being. The only Son who has now returned to the bosom of the Father has made the Father known in the life and actions of Jesus. He brought grace and truth, but he did not receive a universal welcome.

> He was in the world, and the world was made through him, yet the world knew him not. He came to his own home, and his own people received him not. But to all who received him, who believed in his name, he gave power to become children of God; who were born, not of the will of the flesh nor of the will of man, but of God. (John 1:10-13)

11/Remaking the Puzzle

Step 3: The Emerging Picture

> *Jesus said to him, "Have you believed because you have seen me? Blessed are those who have not seen and yet believe."* (John 20:29)

FRAGMENTS OF THE PICTURE

The Gospels of Matthew, Mark, Luke, and John are the main source of our knowledge about Jesus, but they are not the only source. There are many scattered references to Jesus in Roman writers, Josephus, the rabbis, the apocryphal gospels, and even the Qur'an. The reader who wants to follow this up will find the evidence set forth and discussed in F. F. Bruce's *Jesus and Christian Origins Outside the New Testament* (Grand Rapids: Eerdmans, 1974). This material throws some interesting sidelights on our knowledge of Jesus. We shall refer to it later on. But when all is said and done, our main source remains the four Gospels.

Paul's View of Jesus. It is often said that the Gospels were written late—after the letters of Paul. It is even argued that Paul was not interested in the life of Jesus but only in his theology of the cross and resurrection, and that is what matters for us today. In support of this argument appeal is made to Paul's declaration to the Corinthian church: "For I decided to know nothing among you except Jesus Christ and him crucified" (1 Corinthians 2:2). In my view, Paul's words mean the exact opposite. The only Christ he was interested in was the Christ who was crucified—the one we know about from the Gospels that tell us how he came to be crucified. A Christianity that has lost contact with the historical Jesus is not Christianity at all.

At one time Paul himself was in favor of eradicating the church (1 Corinthians 15:9; Acts 9:1-4). But his encounter with the risen Christ on the Damascus road changed all that. On his conversion he dedicated the rest of his life to preaching Jesus Christ. Paul's letters to the various churches do not pretend to give a complete picture of what Christianity is all about. Rather, they were written to clear up particular misconceptions in particular places. Paul was trying to get people to see the right implications of their new-found faith and to avoid the wrong ones. His letters themselves *presuppose* that faith.

It was not only for companionship that Paul took with him colleagues like Mark and Luke. They were men who either had firsthand experience themselves of the people and events connected with Jesus or who had dedicated themselves to recording the story of Jesus. John Mark of Jerusalem went with Barnabas and Paul on Paul's first missionary journey (Acts 12:25; 13:13). Luke was evidently with Paul in his later years (Colossians 4:14; 2 Timothy 4:11). In other words, wherever Paul went, he took with him somebody who could fill in the story of Jesus and so complement his own teaching.

The Date of the Gospels. There is much to be said for the view that Luke wrote Luke and Acts at a time when Paul was in Rome awaiting trial, or shortly afterward. As the opening words of the two books suggest, the Gospel according to Luke and the Acts of the Apostles present a two-volume apologia for the Christian faith. It traces the spread of the faith from before Jesus was born until Paul's house arrest in Rome. If the Book of Acts was written sometime in the sixties, the earlier volume, the Gospel of Luke, must have been written already. This may have been only a matter of weeks. Moreover, Luke mentions earlier narratives that others wrote and also eyewitnesses and ministers of the word who gave him material (Luke 1:1-2). If these narratives included Mark—and most scholars agree that Luke did use Mark—Mark's Gospel must have been written earlier still.

In short, we have to reckon with the possibility that Mark's Gospel and also Luke's were written within a generation of Jesus' death and that eyewitnesses who were still alive provided material through the much-maligned but valuable traditional Jewish method of learning by rote. But to explore these questions would take us too far afield. This much, however, may be said. As the late J. A. T. Robinson argued in his *Redating the New Testament* (Philadelphia: Westminster, 1976), it makes sense to date the Gospels before A.D. 70. For in that year Jerusalem fell to the Romans. It was an event of the greatest significance both to Judaism and to the church, and yet there is no clear mention of it in the New Testament. In the Gospels it is prophesied as a future event.

All this may seem to have taken us some way from the question of miracles. The point of this detour has been to outline the time frame in which the Gospels were written and to indicate some links between the records and the events they describe.

Special Problems. In the last two chapters we have seen something of the place given to the miracles of Jesus in the four Gospels. I have not attempted to explore the kind of setting that scholars envisage for the original readers of the Gospels. In recent years there has been much discussion of the points made by the different Gospel writers and the lessons they were trying to draw out of their stories for their readers. Such an exercise is interesting but highly conjectural. In any case we need to get clear what the stories themselves are saying before we can attempt to reconstruct the beliefs and the sociological situation of the readers of the stories.

We have not been able to explore in detail the interpretation of particular miracle stories. Some cause special problems. What about the coin in the fish's mouth? Did Jesus really turn water into wine? Is not the story of the Gerasene swine, to say the least, bizarre and grotesque? I have looked at different interpretations of these stories in my more technical book *Miracles and the Critical Mind*. Readers who want to follow this through will find there details of current research on the subject of miracles. Discussion of the individual miracle stories requires more time and attention than can be given in a general survey like the present book. But one or two comments are in order here.

The story of the coin in the fish's mouth is told in Matthew 17:24-27. Some scholars do not even regard it as a miracle story. There is no violation of the natural order. It seems to belong to what we earlier called the coincidence or contingency concept of miracle. In the background of the incident is Jesus' relationship to the Jewish law. It is focused by the question: Should Jesus and his followers pay the temple tax? Jesus could have claimed exemption on the grounds that he and his disciples were engaged in God's service. But the collectors were not rabbis capable of determining this. To save them from embarrassment and also to avoid drawing on funds otherwise committed to God's service, Jesus directed Peter, the former fisherman, to an item of lost property that (in Jewish law) the finder could keep. For no one could establish ownership of a coin in a fish's mouth. The fish in question was probably a scaleless catfish, an omnivorous predator that no Jewish fisherman would have attempted to catch. The story has obvious ramifications for the followers of Jesus in determining what their attitude should be to Jewish law.

The story about the water changed into wine at the wedding feast at Cana occurs in John 2:1-11. Some scholars have suggested that the whole story was adopted from the cult of the wine-god Dionysus, and tales like that of a temple fountain on the island of Andros running with wine. But John's Gospel contains little to suggest that the author was seriously concerned to demonstrate the superiority of Jesus over the pagan wine-god. The event in the Gospel was one of a kind. It was not repeated or continuous as in the Dionysus stories.

John's Gospel has a very Jewish background, and it is from Jewish wedding customs that we obtain further light on this story. It was Jewish practice to provide gifts according to rank and status, part of which were devoted to the feast itself. The unforeseen appearance of the disciples at the wedding put a strain on the resources at the feast and were a source of embarrassment to the bridegroom. Jesus' provision of the wine both met his obligations as a guest and avoided causing embarrassment to the groom.

The episode concerning the Gerasene swine is recorded in Matthew 8:28-34, Mark 5:1-20, and Luke 8:26-39. The issues are complex and the account contains overtones of many Old Testament themes. To the Jews pigs were unclean animals. In the background of the story are hints of the practice of bestiality. In the pagan world pigs were sacrificed to all gods except Aphrodite. Pigs were used for expiation. They could be used as decoys for demons. The pigs in the story were destined for sacrifice, the majority to idols or demons. Under normal circumstances Jews were held responsible if they caused the destruction of the property of other people. But animals affected by bestiality were to be destroyed (Leviticus 20:15-16). Objects affected by idol worship were also to be destroyed. In the circumstances Jesus was not liable for blame in the destruction of the animals. He had in fact performed a righteous act.

In making these points I have drawn on the research of J. D. M. Derrett, who until recently was Professor of Oriental Laws in the University of London. His discussion of the coin in the fish's mouth and the wedding at Cana are contained in his book *Law in the New Testament* (London: Darton, Longman and Todd, 1970). His study of the Gerasene demoniac is printed in *Studia Biblica 1978: II. Papers on the*

Gospels, ed. E. A. Livingstone (Sheffield: Journal for the Study of the New Testament. Supplement Series, 2, 1980). Professor Derrett's Jewish background and unrivaled expertise in matters of oriental law and customs shed new light not only on the miracle stories but on many other sayings and events in the Gospels.

I am not saying that the points I have just made solve at a stroke the questions surrounding these stories. By themselves these points do not guarantee the stories as historical events. Neither am I saying that this is all that is to be said about them. I think, for example, that in the background of the story of the wedding at Cana and the feeding stories is the theme of Psalm 104. The Lord provides food and drink. It is he who in the last resort provides "wine to gladden the heart of man" (Psalm 104:15). Isaiah 55:1 gives the invitation to come and buy wine without price! The story in John 2 is like an acted parable. As with most of the other parables, it is up to the reader to discern its meaning. The story prompts the thought that the Son is doing what the Father does. It also prepares the reader for Jesus' declaration, " 'I am the true vine, and my Father is the vinedresser' " (John 15:1). But this links up with another Old Testament theme, namely, that Israel is the vine (Isaiah 5; Psalm 80).

In short, I am suggesting that there is more to the miracle stories than meets the eye. They cannot simply be dismissed as the product of pious imagination coupled with a desire to make Jesus outdo anything that a pagan deity could do. They are presented as events—as distinct from parables. And yet they have parabolic significance. They are acted signs. To understand the sign, we need to understand the sign language.

Professor Derrett's concluding remarks on the Gerasene demoniac are well worth pondering.

> The episode teaches that, so far as demon-possession was concerned, Jesus was an acknowledged expert, who saw the subjective condition of *possession* as intrinsically hostile to

his mission wherever it occurred, whether amongst nominally observant Jews or lapsed Jews (as this one probably was), or gentiles. The mind not prepared to welcome the Holy Spirit, and to take it as a final and exclusive guide is territory into which the ambassadors of the Kingdom of Heaven must penetrate, land which they must claim for their Sovereign. We do not know whether Jesus contemplated the human mind *exempt* from the propensity to be possessed (cf. Matt. 12:45), or indeed whether such a mind exists or will exist. (*Studia Biblica 1978*, p. 70)

THE PROBABILITY OF THE PICTURE

We have to acknowledge that miracles are improbable. If they were not improbable, they would not be miracles. But we cannot solve the problem simply by saying that. Some improbable things we may rationally believe, and other improbable things we rationally reject. I believe that Jesus was a historical figure who performed miracles. I do not believe in myths about the gods coming down to earth and performing various acts prior to resuming their former status. What is the difference? Have I any good, rational reasons for thinking that Jesus really did the kind of things that he is said to have done?

My answer to these questions turns on what I have already said in Chapters 3–6. To start with, we have to reckon with the fact that life itself is unpredictable. A detached observer could predict that from Monday through Friday throughout the year I will leave for my office around 7:45 a.m. (give or take a minute or two) and get there fifteen minutes later. It is an established pattern of my life. The observer could predict how much coffee I will drink in a normal working day. But no observer could predict which of all the coffee beans grown in the world I would use to make any given cup of coffee.

Prediction based on probability has its place in dealing with the broad patterns of regular behavior and natural occurrences. In terms of probability based on our day-to-day experience of the world, we would have to say that the miracle stories of the New Testament are so strange and alien that they are unlikely to be true. We could not rule out their possibility. But we would have to say that they are so unlikely that we would need a great deal of counterargument to convince us of their truth.

But to argue like this would be to argue like the King of Siam who refused to believe in ice because he had no experience of it. This brings us back to what I have called our frame of reference. We view things in the light of our past experience and our present understanding of reality, which together form our frame of reference. As our experience grows and our understanding is enlarged, our frame of reference expands. In the last analysis our approach to the miracle stories will depend on our frame of reference. In turn, our approach to them will itself become part of our frame of reference.

Taken in isolation, any given miracle story could be dismissed as absurd and incredible. But within a frame of reference that includes belief in the God of the Bible, the personal Creator, actively being involved in human affairs, the possibility of miracles is feasible. We do not have to imagine a God-of-the-gaps in nature. But we have to see miracles in the context of the personal Creator and Redeemer. We do not have to think of miracles as violations of nature. They become much more feasible if we think of them as what C. S. Lewis called Miracles of the Old Creation—God's ordering of the powers of nature for the benefit of humankind—and Miracles of the New Creation—the manifestation of God's new order in our present order.

In the last analysis, the reason why I believe in Jesus as a miracle worker and why I reject as myths stories about the ancient gods visiting earth in human form is bound up with my frame of reference. Classical mythology does not make sense to me as history within my frame of reference, but stories about Jesus do.

A Neglected Argument. In the course of this book we have, however, noticed one argument in favor of Jesus as a miracle worker that does not depend upon the say-so of the early Christians. It turns upon the attitude of Jesus' opponents. Admittedly, the primary source for our knowledge of those attitudes is Christian writings. But they are not without external corroboration. In Chapters 8 and 9 we looked at Deuteronomy 13 and other passages from the Old Testament law. We noted their instructions on what to do with a worker of signs and wonders who leads the people astray. The answer is, kill him—and so remove the evil out of the midst of God's people. I argued that this instruction helps to explain the attitude of the Pharisees. They saw Jesus as someone who was leading the people astray from God and the truth about God expressed in the law of Moses. They saw him as a wonder worker whose wonders went hand-in-hand with his teaching. They did not consider seriously the unthinkable—that God himself might be present in the words, works, and person of Jesus. Instead, they saw no alternative but to get rid of Jesus.

All this happened very early in Jesus' ministry. It took place long before Peter confessed Jesus as the Christ and attention became focused on Jesus as the messiah. To the Pharisees the activity of Jesus was satanic. What was satanic to the Pharisees was in the eyes of the Gospel writers the activity of the Holy Spirit.

If this line of argument is correct, several things follow. First of all, we cannot separate the teaching of Jesus from his activity as a worker of signs and wonders. Just as the signs of a prophet cannot be separated from the message of the prophet, the signs of Jesus cannot be separated from his teaching.

Secondly, the traditions about Jesus' supernatural healings and exorcisms belong (at least substantially) to Palestinian soil. The decision to kill Jesus was initially bound up with his activity as a miracle worker. If he had been merely a sabbath-breaker, he could only have been excommunicated.

The decision to kill Jesus at this point could have been justified for the God-fearing, law-abiding Pharisees only by the teaching of the law itself.

Thirdly, these traditions go back to the earliest strata of Christian belief about Jesus. It is not as if the first Christians believed in a simple, meek and mild Jesus who taught timeless truths about loving God and loving our fellow human beings, and who did nothing else. It is not as if the miracle stories were invented later by Christians facing persecution in order to cheer each other up when the going got rough. The miracles themselves were the initial cause of the persecution. Because Jesus was believed to be engaged in the occult, steps were taken against him from the time that he healed the man with the withered hand.

Fourthly, those scholars are on the wrong track who think that the Gospel picture of Jesus is borrowed from "divine man" stories in the ancient pagan world. For some years the idea has been tossed about that the ancient stories of Jesus' mighty acts have been modeled on the exploits of the so-called "divine men" of antiquity. To put it bluntly, the implication is that these stories were motivated by the same impulses behind the song in *Annie Get Your Gun*, "Anything you can do I can do better." Anything a "divine man" or a pagan deity could do, Jesus could do better. But if the initial opposition to Jesus was prompted by his healings and exorcisms, the ground is undercut from this argument. To say the very least, a hard core of miracle stories were circulating around Jesus from the beginning.

Furthermore, recent scholarship has moved away from the "divine man" idea. Scholars are now saying that the idea of a "divine man" in antiquity is a very broad concept. It does not necessarily mean deification. It could indicate a holy man, a man of God, or an extraordinary man. Moreover, there is no clear tendency to link "divine men" with miracles or to authenticate their claims by appealing to miracles.

Corroboration. The construction I have placed on the Phari-sees' motives is given corroboration from Jewish sources. First of all, there is the Mishnah, the authoritative collection of legal and procedural teaching, based on oral tradition. Though arranged and edited early in the third century, it preserves earlier Pharisaic and rabbinic teaching. In importance it stands next to Scripture in Jewish thinking.

The Mishnah tractate *Sanhedrin* prescribes death for (among others) "the blasphemer and the idolater, . . . he that has a familiar spirit and the soothsayer, and he that profanes the Sabbath . . . and he that beguiles [others to idolatry], and he that leads [a whole town astray], and the sorcerer and a stubborn and rebellious son" (7:4). The Tractate goes on to say: " 'He that profanes the Sabbath' [is liable, after warning, to death by stoning] if he committed an act which renders him liable to Extirpation if he acted wantonly, or to a Sin-offering if he acted in error" (7:8). *Sanhedrin* 10:4 explicitly mentions Deuteronomy 13:13 in dealing with "beguilers" of a city and discusses under what circumstances they are to be put to death.

The tradition that Jesus was a sorcerer who led Israel astray is preserved in the Babylonian Talmud. The Talmud was a later work that contained exposition of the Mishnah.

> Jesus was hanged on Passover Eve. Forty days previously a herald had cried, "He is led out for stoning, because he has practiced sorcery and led Israel astray and enticed them into apostasy. Whosoever has anything to say in his defense, let him come and declare it." As nothing was brought forward in his defense, he was hanged on Passover Eve. (*Sanhedrin* 43a; see F. F. Bruce, *Jesus and Christian Origins,* p. 56)

This is followed by the comment of a third-century rabbi that contains an allusion to Deuteronomy 13:9.

> Ulla said: "Would you believe that any defense would have been so zealously sought for him? He was a deceiver, and the All-merciful says: 'You shall not spare him, neither shall you conceal him.' It was different with Jesus, for he was near to kingship."

This last point made by Ulla may have meant that the reason why grounds were sought for not proceeding against Jesus was that he was influential. It might also mean that it was because he was related to royalty, in reference to his descent from David. These statements may reflect the hostility that had developed between Christians and Jews over a period of time. The reference to stoning and the herald may have been an attempt to rewrite history by bringing the account into line with prescribed practices. Nevertheless, there is a convergence of sources. The Gospel accounts and Jewish teaching point in the same direction concerning the original, official Jewish opposition to Jesus.

It may be asked, "If this is so, why does this motive not figure more prominently in the accounts of the trial of Jesus?" My answer is threefold.

First of all, lingering echoes of the charge of deception run through the Gospels. In Matthew's account of Jesus' trial before the Sanhedrin the high priest used language that is evocative of exorcism: " 'I adjure [exhorkizō] you by the living God, tell us if you are the Christ, the Son of God' " (Matthew 26:63). (Note the use of horkizō in connection with exorcism in Mark 5:7 and Acts 19:13.) In his passion Jesus was mockingly invited to prophesy and also seek miraculous escape. The description by the guard at the tomb of Jesus as a deceiver (Greek planos) who prophesied his resurrection (Matthew 27:63) also contains echoes of the earlier charge.

Secondly, the Pharisees were hindered in making the charge stick. Jesus demonstrated the self-contradictory character of the charge. The exorcisms and healings were patently not the work of Satan. Jesus did not oblige his adversaries by performing a sign before their very eyes that they could take as clear proof of his guilt as a sorcerer. The Jews retained their suspicions but could not get very far with the charge.

Thirdly, events changed somewhat after Peter's confession that Jesus was the Christ. From that point onward Jesus' ministry was directed toward Jerusalem. It culminated in his entry on the first Palm Sunday, the cleansing of the temple, and his subsequent ministry in the temple. This was the manifestation of his messianic office as the Spirit-anointed Christ. Because of what were seen to be his blasphemous, messianic claims, Jesus was finally condemned. But a thread of continuity runs through it all. It is supplied by the Spirit's anointing of Jesus as the messianic Son. To Jesus' enemies it was an evil spirit, but to the followers of Jesus it was the divine anointing of the Son of God by the Spirit of God.

WHAT SORT OF PICTURE IS EMERGING?

The Actions of Jesus Were Signs. They were signs of the Kingdom. If it is by the Spirit of God that Jesus casts out demons, then the Kingdom of God has come (Matthew 12:28; Luke 11:20). They were also signs of Jesus as the Son of God. But we underrate the miracle stories if we think of them simply as *external* proofs of the truth of the teaching and authority of Jesus. They are not external to the message. They do not function like a guarantee that is quite separate from the product itself. They are not like a guarantee that comes with a washing machine or a TV set. Guarantees of this kind are pieces of paper. They are valuable, but we can put them away until they are needed. We do not expect the piece of paper to do the washing or show our favorite programs.

The acts of Jesus were in the tradition of prophetic signs. They are part of the message itself. They embody the message like an acted parable. They embody the saving action of God in Christ. They are not the sole embodiment of that action, but they are forms of the embodiment of that action.

The Gospels Present the Miracle Stories within the Overall Context of the Kingdom and the Baptism of the Holy Spirit. The Kingdom of God is the reign of God. Through Jesus, the messianic King, the reign of God is becoming a reality. There are many aspects to the reign of God. It involves the conquest of Satan, the demons, and sin. Jesus has bound Satan and has begun to release those who are in his power. Jesus, as the Son of God, does this in the power of the Spirit of God. He liberates men and women from bondage. His work constitutes a baptism of the Holy Spirit in which he frees people from sin, the evil spirits, and all uncleanness, and consecrates them to God. Through his action they can be true human beings, living the life that the loving Father intends them to live.

Not everyone has the same need. The paralytic who was let down through the roof was unable to walk. His need was linked with sins that needed divine forgiveness (Mark 2:5; cf. John 5:15). But not all illness is linked with sin. Sometimes illness is traced to Satan's bondage (e.g., Luke 13:16; Acts 10:38), but explicit connections of illness with Satan are rare. In John 9:3 Jesus sweeps away the disciples' suggestion that the blindness of the man born blind was due to his own sin or to that of his parents.

Physical Illness and Demonic Possession. Although exorcism and healing are frequently mentioned together and in some cases the reason for the sickness is attributed to possession, the Gospels do not regard all illness as due to demons. In Jesus' dealings with people, a certain pattern seems to emerge. In dealing with the possessed, Jesus cast out demons by his word. In dealing with the physically sick, Jesus healed with a touch. Perhaps there are exceptions to this rule. Jesus healed the paralytic in Mark 2 by his word, but here the root trouble was the man's need of forgiveness. He commanded the man with the withered hand to stretch forth his hand (Mark 3:5), but here too there was a special need. The man needed to do this. Jesus rebuked the fever that gripped Simon's mother-in-law (Luke 4:39). But elsewhere, as Luke 4:40-41 observes, Jesus laid hands on those who were sick with various diseases, and rebuked the spirits.

Perhaps we are meant to see in all this that Jesus dealt with human needs in the most appropriate way. Where the root of the trouble was personal, he addressed it in a personal way. Where the root of the trouble was physical, he dealt with it in a physical way. In Jesus' parable of the Good Samaritan (Luke 10:25-36), the man in need is restored by normal care and attention.

The laying on of hands may well have had a special significance. It was connected in Christian thought and practice with the bestowal of the Spirit (Acts 8:14-19; 19:6) and consecration (Acts 13:1-3). The expressions "hand of God" and "finger of God" were ways of speaking about the Spirit of God or God in action (Exodus 7:4-5; 8:19; 9:3, 15; 31:18; Deuteronomy 9:10; Psalm 8:3). Thus, underlying the act of touching with his hands is the suggestion of bestowing the Spirit. But there is also another thought. In touching the leper (Mark 1:41) and the body of Jairus's daughter (Mark 5:41), and in being touched by the woman with the flow of blood (Mark 5:27), Jesus became unclean from the standpoint of the law. But instead of becoming unclean himself, he bestowed restoration, life, and cleanness on the recipient of his touch.

There is heated debate among scholars whether the description of demon possession in the Gospels is really an ancient way of describing mental illness or whether the Gospel writers mean to say that demons are real in their own sort of way. The matter is clearly one for careful, ongoing research into the Gospel accounts. My own reply is along the following lines.

First, there seems to be a real difference between mental illness, as psychologists and psychiatrists describe it today, and the cases described in the Gospels. The forms of mental illness known to us today are more numerous and more extensive than the cases described in the Gospels.

Secondly, we should not rule out the possibility that some of the cases so described in the Gospels were cases of mental illness. But neither should we rule out the possibility that certain cases of mental illness may be rooted in possession. Those who suffer in this way require psychotherapy, spiritual care, and the attention of an exorcist who knows what he is doing.

Thirdly, we need to note the case of the boy in Mark 9:14-27, Matthew 17:14-18, and Luke 9:37-43. The boy was suffering from convulsions with symptoms that have been diagnosed as epilepsy. But there are different kinds of epilepsy, and the diagnosis of epilepsy does not rule out possession as the cause. If the boy had been suffering from a certain type of epilepsy, we might have expected Jesus to have healed him by an act of healing instead of treating his disease as a case of possession.

Not Magic. In short, there seem to be in the Gospels certain lines of demarcation. Some illnesses are physical, while others are spiritual. The Gospels present Jesus as the one who gives life and also as the vanquisher of the powers of evil. He is the one who has power to overcome the natural and spiritual enemies of humankind. But he does not do this by means of magic. His word of command is not magical incantation. Jesus did not use unintelligible formulae like "Abracadabra." It was not as if the right use of the right words had power in itself to manipulate evil spirits. Granted that the Gospels preserve utterances like *"Talitha cumi"* (Mark 5:41) and *"Ephphatha"* (Mark 7:34). But these were not meaningless formulae. Instead, they were Aramaic words that belonged to the everyday language of the hearers. In both instances Mark provides a translation for the benefit of his readers. *Talitha cumi* means "Little girl, I say to you, arise." *Ephphatha* means "Be opened."

What is striking about both these instances is the fact that the people addressed could not hear the words! Jairus's daughter had been pronounced dead, and *"Ephphatha"* was addressed to a deaf man with an impediment in his speech. In other words, these commands of Jesus were like the creative speech-acts of God. They bring about what they say in the very act of saying it.

No Techniques. Although Jesus laid hands on people and on occasion is said to have touched the blind and deaf with spittle (Mark 7:33; 8:23; John 9:6), he did not have what could be called a technique. As distinct from those who practice psychotherapy, he made no preparations and did not have repeated consultations. He called those who were healed to praise and prayer, and he prayed himself. He performed no miracle in his own interest. He made no attempt to call on supernatural power to preserve himself or deliver himself from suffering and death. Jesus' healing work was not part of an evangelistic strategy designed to pull in the crowds and soften them up for the message he wanted to deliver. It was not a ploy in the tactic of "power evangelism," but was done for its own sake. It was done out of compassion in order to meet human needs (Matthew 4:23-24; 8:17, 25; 15:30; Mark 1:41; 2:17; 9:22-23; 10:47; Acts 10:38). The healings and the exorcisms of Jesus belong to the baptism of the Holy Spirit, in which Jesus cleansed, made whole, and consecrated men and women for the life of the Kingdom of God.

Healing and Faith. In all this, faith plays an important part. It is not like magic, where the personal character and attitudes of those concerned play no real part and where the manipulation of power by the right use of formulae and procedures is what matters. Jesus told the woman who touched him, " 'Daughter, your faith has made you well; go in peace, and be healed of your disease' " (Mark 5:34). Jesus' actions are the embodiment of the gospel. They are the gospel in action. Men and women are being saved from that which is destroying them. They are being restored to a life of faith and fellowship with God. In addressing those whom he restores as "son" and "daughter" (Mark 2:5; 5:34; cf. Matthew 9:2) it is as if God is fulfilling his promise through Jesus, " 'I will be your God, and you shall be my people' " (cf. Exodus 6:7; Leviticus 26:12; Jeremiah 7:23; 31:33; 2 Corinthians 6:10; Hebrews 8:10; Revelation 21:3, etc.). It is as if they are being summoned and restored to the life of the covenant people of God.

The great Swiss theologian Karl Barth has observed: "The distinctive feature of the New Testament faith in miracles is that it was faith in Jesus and therefore faith in God as the faithful and merciful God of the covenant with Israel; and in this way and as such it was this confidence in His power" (*Church Dogmatics* [Edinburgh: T. & T. Clark, 1958], III/2, p. 236). But faith is not something mechanical and therefore will not always produce a miracle. Faith is a personal relationship. It is trust in God.

In some instances faith is the precondition of Jesus' response (Matthew 8:10; 9:18, 22, 28; 14:31; 17:20; Mark 2:4-5; 4:40; 5:34, 36; 11:23; Luke 7:50; 17:6). In John's account of the healing of the blind man the healing itself leads to faith (John 9:35-38). Other acts of Jesus either produce faith or are expected to produce faith (John 10:37-38; 12:37; 20:31; cf. 4:48; 6:30; Matthew 11:4-5, 20-21; Luke 24:19). But this too is not automatic. Jesus' actions also provoke opposition (Matthew 12:24-29; Mark 3:22-27; Luke 11:15-22; John 7:20; 8:48; 10:20). John presents the raising of Lazarus as the crowning event, one that led the council to resolve on Jesus' execution (John 11:47-48). Jesus steadfastly refused the request to do signs for the sake of providing credentials for faith in him (Matthew 12:38-42; 16:1-4; Mark 8:11-12; Luke 11:16, 29-32; John 6:30-34).

The Nature Miracles. Unlike the healings and the exorcisms, the so-called nature miracles of Jesus were not ongoing, repeated events. The Gospels give accounts of two feedings of the multitudes, one account of changing water into wine, one instance of the stilling of the storm, and one instance of walking on the waves. Only in John's account of the feeding of the multitude is attention drawn to the response of the people (John 6:14). The events are essentially signs for the disciples. The situations that prompted them were not necessarily life-threatening. What they have in common is that they focus attention on Jesus as the one who does things within the time and space framework of the disciples' experience. In the Old Testament God is said to do this for his people in general.

What Distinguishes Jesus' Miracles from Those of Others? What sets Jesus apart? The Old Testament tells of the signs and wonders wrought by Moses and the miraculous acts of Elijah and Elisha. In the New Testament there are reports of healings and exorcisms by the apostles and others (Acts 2:43; 3:1-20; 4:16, 22, 30; 5:12; 8:6, 13; 14:3, 8; 16:16-18; 19:11-12; 20:9-12; Romans 15:18-19; 1 Corinthians 2:4; 12:28-30; 2 Corinthians 12:12; Galatians 3:5; Hebrews 2:4). But there are also the signs and wonders of the false prophet and the false Christ (Matthew 24:24; Mark 13:22), and there are signs that are satanic and demonic (2 Thessalonians 2:9; Revelation 13:13-14; 16:14; 19:20). In neither the Old nor the New Testament is the mere supernaturalness of the sign or wonder sufficient in itself to accredit the one who performs it.

How Are People Expected to Tell the True from the False? What is so special about the healings, the exorcisms, the miracles, and the signs of Jesus? My answer is along these lines. All true miracles are "in character." They are in character with the work and words of God, as we know them from other parts of God's revelation. As such, they bring glory to God (John 7:18; 8:50). It is characteristic of the magician and the false prophet to draw attention to himself. He seeks to promote himself. It is characteristic of Jesus' works that they point people to the Father.

What Are the Miracle Stories Saying? When we look at the works of the apostles and the early Christians, a pattern begins to emerge. They were not done in the name of the apostle or of whoever happened to do them. They were done in the name of Jesus and in the power of the Holy Spirit. This was not a magical power that could be bought and manipulated, as Simon Magus imagined (Acts 8:14-24). It had to do with being in Christ and perceiving the Spirit of God through Christ. But neither Christ nor the Spirit is an autonomous figure. Jesus Christ is the Son of the Father who is anointed by the Spirit of the Father. In other words, the works of the apostles and the early Christians point us to Christ and the Spirit, who in turn point us to the Father. Or to put it the other way around, the Father manifests himself through his Son in the power of his Spirit.

Sometimes the works of Jesus are depicted as his works (e.g., John 5:17, 19), sometimes they are presented as the work of the Spirit (e.g., Matthew 12:28; Luke 11:20), and sometimes they are attributed to the Father (e.g., John 14:10). In the light of the picture of Jesus that has emerged in the last three chapters, we are not to think that some works were done by Jesus, others were done by the Spirit, and others again were the work of the Father. Rather, we are being given glimpses of the threefoldness of the one God. We are being pointed to what the Christian church calls the Trinity, to the God who always is and acts in this threefoldness.

In the past Christian apologists have argued for the divinity of Christ along two lines of argument. On the one hand, he did miracles that only a divine being could do. On the other hand, he fulfilled prophecy in a way only God could arrange. In the light of our study, this argument needs to be reformulated. For one thing, there are not really two separate lines. In fact, miracles and prophecy converge. For the miracles of Jesus were not all-purpose miracles that simply impressed people by their sheer supernatural power. They were miracles that fulfilled prophecy. The evangelists saw in Jesus the fulfilment of Isaiah 35:5-6. When John the Baptist inquired whether Jesus really was " 'He who is to come,' " he was reminded of this passage (Matthew 11:5; Luke 7:22). The point is not simply that Jesus fulfilled prophecy, but that the works that he did are the works that belong to the time of the messiah.

But this is not all. At his baptism the "voice from heaven" identified Jesus with the anointed son of Psalm 2 and the chosen beloved of Isaiah 42:1. The latter passage is seen as being fulfilled by Jesus' works in Matthew 12:18-21. Isaiah 61:1-2 speaks of the anointed one and his mission. This passage too is seen as being fulfilled by Jesus' person and works (Matthew 11:5; Luke 4:18-19; 7:22). If we study these Old Testament prophecies, we discover that the one who achieves this is either God, the Holy One of Israel, or the servant on whom God has put his Spirit. In other words, we are again pointed to the God who in Christian theology is identified as the Trinity.

The Messianic Secret. I think that this point is underlined by what scholars call "the messianic secret." This topic has been heatedly discussed for many years now. It arises out of the fact that Jesus repeatedly commanded the demons to be silent (e.g., Mark 1:25) and forbade those whom he healed to say anything about it (e.g., Mark 2:44). He even charged his disciples to tell no one that he was the Christ (Mark 8:30).

This is not the place to review the various passages and arguments. My own explanation is along these lines. Jesus' action could well be explained as the observance of an ancient Jewish tradition that no man had the right to claim messiahship until he had fulfilled the deeds of the messiah. But there was a special reason why Jesus did not want the testimony of the possessed—even though they correctly discerned who he was, " 'the Holy One of God' " (Mark 1:24) or the " 'Son of God' " (Mark 3:11). If he had acknowledged it, his enemies could well have claimed with some semblance of truth that Jesus was in league with Satan and the demons. Jesus steadfastly refused to have any dealings with the powers of evil. But he also knew the dangers of confessing him and following him. He wanted people to acknowledge him freely of their own accord. They had to see him for who he was, and they had to count the cost not least because of the way he himself was viewed by his opponents. To confess Jesus was a dangerous thing, especially at a time when his enemies were convinced that he was possessed by Satan.

If the interpretation that I have given in the past three chapters is correct, the messianic secret was not simply a Jesus-secret. It was also a Holy Spirit-secret. For as we have seen, "Christ" means "anointed." It poses the question "Anointed by whom?" Jesus' enemies gave in effect the answer "Anointed by Satan" or "Possessed by Satan." The Gospels give us the answer that Jesus was anointed by the Holy Spirit, and that what he did was done in the power of the Spirit. The title "Christ" contains an implicit allusion to the Spirit. To confess Jesus as the Christ is not only to make a statement about Jesus; it is also to make a statement about the Spirit and the Spirit's activity in him.

MIRACLES AND THE TRINITY

Christian belief in the Trinity is not a myth about three gods, a story like that of Zeus and Apollo, or a tale of how the chief god sent one of his children down to earth and how that lesser god after many adventures returned to his former state. To put it in more modern terms, the Bible does not depict the deity like three key players on a baseball team. It is not as if the senior god, the manager in the heavenly dugout, said to one of the players, "It's your turn to bat." It is not as if, when the son had batted away for some time and finally scored the winning run, the manager said to the third player, the Spirit, "Now it's your turn. Keep on going to the end of the age."

The Christian faith has always rejected tritheism. It does not teach belief in three gods who take turns acting. From beginning to end, the Bible is thoroughly monotheistic.

It presents us with the one eternal God in his eternal threefoldness.

How are we to think of this God in his threefoldness? The late Roman Catholic theologian Karl Rahner once made this observation:

> Throughout the Old Testament there runs the basic theme that God is the absolute mystery, whom nobody can see without dying, and that it is nevertheless this God *himself* who conversed with the Fathers through his actions in history. This revealing self-manifestation is, in the Old Testament, mediated mostly . . . by the "Word," which, while causing God to be present in power, also represents him; and by the "Spirit," who helps men to understand and announce the Word. When these two are not active, Yahweh has retreated from his people. When he bestows upon the "holy remnant" his renewed forever victorious mercy, he sent *the* prophet with his Word in the fullness of the Spirit. (The Torah and Wisdom doctrine of sapiential literature is only a more individualistic version of the same conception. It pays less attention to historical development.) God is present in the unity of Word and Spirit. (*The Trinity* [New York: Seabury, 1974], p. 41)

A little earlier in the same book Rahner argues that "A revelation of the Father without the Logos and his incarnation would be like speaking without words" (p. 29). But we might equally well say that a revelation of the Father without his Spirit would be like speaking without breath.

These comments might at first sound cryptic. But they may also hold the key to what the New Testament is saying about miracles and about Jesus. To grasp the point we need to remember two things. On the one hand, the Greek word *logos* means "word," "speech," "reason." It is the term used at the beginning of John's Gospel: "In the beginning was the Word, and the Word was with God, and the Word was God." On the other hand, the word that we translate as "spirit" in the New Testament is the Greek word *pneuma*. Its Hebrew counterpart in the Old Testament is *rûaḥ*. Literally, both of these words mean "wind" and "breath." Both wind and breath symbolize energy and life. The Spirit came as a rushing wind at Pentecost (Acts 2:2). The Spirit in the sense of the divine breath is clearly symbolized in the prophetic sign of the risen Christ, when he breathed on the disciples and said, " 'Receive the Holy Spirit' " (John 20:22).

If we look further back into the Old Testament we find that in Genesis 1 creation is attributed to the Word of God. To adapt the language we have used of Christologies, we could say that Genesis 1 teaches an explicit Word doctrine of creation. At the same time it mentions the Spirit, the wind or breath, of God moving over the face of the waters. Moreover, the account of creation contains an implicit Spirit or breath doctrine. For we cannot speak without breath. When God speaks his Word, he does so by means of his divine breath, the Spirit. Psalm 33:6 spells out the point in the parallelism, "By the word of the LORD the heavens were made, and all their host by the breath of his mouth." From one standpoint, creation is the work of God's Word, the expression of his mind. From another standpoint, it is the work of his breath. Breath is the vital power of life; it is also the means by which words are articulated.

The same basic idea is expressed in the New Testament in the observation that all Scripture is God-breathed or inspired (Greek *theopneustos*; 2 Timothy 3:16). In other words, the Word of God is articulated by the Spirit or breath of God. We cannot have the Word without the Spirit or the Spirit without the Word.

Our study of miracles is pointing us in the same direction. From one standpoint, the miracles of Jesus are the work of the Spirit or the divine breath in and through him. From another standpoint, they are wrought by the Word of God that he uttered and that, according to John, was made flesh in him. From yet another standpoint, both these activities were the work of the Father. For the Spirit is the Spirit of the Father and the Word is the Word of the Father.

In all this, Jesus did not for one moment cease to be

a real, live human being. He remained a human being, but was what he was because of God's being in him. If we ask how God could be in him, the answer that John's Gospel gives is this: "The Word became flesh and dwelt among us, full of grace and truth; we have beheld his glory, glory as of the only Son from the Father" (John 1:14). And if we ask how this could be, the Nicene Creed sums up the reply in the words, "And was incarnate by the Holy Spirit of the Virgin Mary, and was made man." The Word became flesh through the Holy Spirit. As such Jesus was the unique Son of God. Whatever the term "Son of God" might have meant in Israel as a designation for the king, it is redefined by Jesus. And the things he did are recorded by the Gospel writers as signs that we might believe that Jesus is the Christ, the Son of God, and that believing we might have life in his name.

III / Can We Expect Miracles Today?

12 / Health and Wealth for All?

We must not box God in (George, former cancer patient).

Up to this point we have been looking at questions people ask about miracles. "Are they really credible?" "What is the point of the miracle stories?" "What are we to make of Jesus?" I have given my answers, and with them I am brought back to the other set of questions with which I began.

"Should I expect miracles today?"
"If Jesus healed people then, how about now?"
"If I have enough faith, will I be healed?"

To me these questions are not just academic. Most of my professional life has been spent in the world of academics. But I have been an ordained minister for still longer. As a professor in a major seminary I am engaged in training men and women for ministry—ordained and lay. At the same time I am the Associate minister in a suburban church outside Los Angeles, where I am actively involved in the church's ministry week in and week out.

The questions that the miracle stories about Jesus raise for us do not simply belong to the realms of philosophy and academic theology. They challenge our faith, our commitment, and our whole view of what the Christian life is about. John's Gospel tells us that the signs it reports are recorded "that you may believe that Jesus is the Christ, the Son of God, and that believing you may have life in his name" (John 20:31). What is this "life" that John is talking about?

It is here that we get into difficulties. When we look around at the literature in the Christian bookstores, the programs on religious TV, the courses, seminars, and workshops that are offered, not to mention the regular Sunday preaching in churches, we find a bewildering smorgasbord of competing claims. Some preachers preach a gospel of self-esteem and success. Some go so far as to say that Paul's teaching in 2 Corinthians 8:9 is to be taken literally. Jesus "became poor, so that by his poverty you might become rich." It is God's plan, they tell us, that the really believing, born-again man and woman should be rich and successful. The same is said about health. If we really believe, then God will deliver us from pain and disease. After all, it is God's plan that we should be "whole." "Wholeness" belongs to salvation. It is the birthright of the born again!

What are we to make of statements like these? There is no way in which the ordinary layperson can survey all the arguments and evidence. The list of books on the subject of healing is enormous. Even so, to assess the claims and counterclaims would require an expertise in medicine, psychology, and anthropology, not to mention theology.

I have listed a number of key books in A Note on Books at the end of the present work. My list makes no pretense at completeness. It may look daunting, but it represents only a cross section of what is available. A good number of these books are written on a popular level. Some of the material is positively anecdotal, telling moving stories with a touch of drama. Depending on how you look at them, you could say that some of the authors are set on winning you over to their point of view. A more generous assessment would be that they are concerned to share the fullness of life that is available to those who believe.

The one clear fact that emerges is that there is no agreement. The advocates of a healing ministry make impressive claims. Their opponents raise questions. Back comes the reply, "Well, you have not really tried it." And so it goes on. What are we to make of the claims and counterclaims?

We can make a start by recognizing that the arguments fall into two basic categories. On the one hand, there is the appeal to experience—the claims that people have been healed supernaturally by faith. On the other hand, there are the theological arguments—the appeals to Scripture that claim that God has given the gift of healing to the church together with a mandate to exercise that gift. We need to look at these two kinds of arguments in turn.

THE APPEAL TO EXPERIENCE

What Do We Mean by "Facts"? When people appeal to experience, they assume that they are appealing to facts. But we need to think a bit about this. What is a fact? *Webster's New Collegiate Dictionary* gives as one of its definitions of a fact: "a piece of information presented as having objective reality." I do not think that many people would want to quarrel with this definition. I certainly would not want to. But notice what it involves.

A fact is not something that we see directly! It is an item of information. It is a construction that we place on something. It is a deduction or an inference. A fact differs from a piece of guesswork or a conjecture in that we claim for it some kind of objective reality. We not only believe that a fact contains information that corresponds to reality; we also believe that it can be *shown* to correspond to reality.

We need to notice two further things about facts. The first is that facts have meaning only within given schemes of interpretation. They need to be seen in terms of a frame of reference. The language of the chemist and the physicist has meaning only within the frames of reference of their respective disciplines. When chemists or physicists look at something from a scientific point of view, they are not looking at the thing in its totality. They are looking at it in terms of their discipline, and they are examining it in terms of the accepted procedures of their discipline.

The second thing that we need to notice about claiming something to be a fact is that we are laying ourselves open to being asked to give our reasons. When we claim that something is a fact, we are saying in effect that certain considerations count within our frame of reference toward substantiating that claim. We are also implying that, if these considerations were not there, we could not and would not make the claim.

Facts and Truth Claims. We cannot have our cake and eat it too. If we want to talk about facts, we have to be prepared to say what counts for and against the facts in question. It is no different from playing a game. The same rules that apply when we score apply equally when our opponents score against us. If we claim that something is a fact, the rules of the game mean that we must be willing to face up not only to the possibility of having to establish our truth claims, but also to the possibility of having them undermined if it should turn out that the considerations underlying them were invalid in some way or other.

What does all this have to do with claims to divine healing? First, it means that we need to recognize that all claims involve interpretation within a frame of reference. If we ascribe a case of healing to divine intervention, we need to recognize that we are construing the events in question in the context of a scheme of beliefs. Secondly, we need to recognize that claims to divine healing involve at least two main frames of reference—the medical frame of reference and the theological frame of reference. Thirdly, it means that if we claim something as a fact of divine healing, we must be prepared to back it up in terms of *both* these frames of reference—or back down.

What then do we make of the claims to divine healing? Certainly there are many claims to healing in the church, both ancient and modern. But many lack detailed documentation. The constructions placed on the testimonies of the early fathers and the medieval church by popular writers are not necessarily the same as those of the trained historian. Although B. B. Warfield did not say the last word on the subject, his book *Miracles: Yesterday and Today, True and False* (reprint Grand Rapids: Eerdmans, 1954) remains a massive indictment of the tenuous character of so many claims to healing through the ages.

Even so, the testimony to healing cannot be dismissed as groundless. What is curious, however, is the vehemence with which some non-Catholics dismiss Roman Catholic claims. This is matched only by the vehemence of die-hard Catholics in dismissing non-Catholic claims. The diehards on both sides find themselves on the same side in dismissing the claims of Christian Science. And the more people relate claims to healing to the truth claims of their theological position, the more they are inclined to leave out of account altogether the claims to supernatural healing in non-Christian religions.

Evidence for Miracles Today. A study of healings associated with the work of the late Kathryn Kuhlman has been made by a medical doctor, H. Richard Casdorph (*The Miracles* [Plainfield, N.J.: Logos International, 1976]). In popular, dramatic language Dr. Casdorph describes cases of cancer, heart disease, arthritis, and massive bleeding. The book contains pictures, including X-rays. The cover depicts a doctor dressed for surgery and bears the words, "A medical doctor says yes to miracles!" The book is dedicated to the memory of Kathryn Kuhlman. Perhaps the most striking feature of the entire book is not the nature of the cases described but the fact that there are only ten of them.

The Roman Catholic Church exercises considerable care and caution in its examination of claims to miraculous healing. In the cases of healings at Lourdes, the Lourdes Medical Bureau has published medical dossiers. Even so, they have provoked the following comment from an expert investigator: "In no case was the evidence really satisfactory, and in certain cases the evidence suggested a perfectly natural alternative explanation" (D. J. West, *Eleven Lourdes Miracles* [London: Duckworth, 1957], p. 97).

Commenting on the way in which miracles in the Roman Catholic Church are linked with the process of beatification and the canonization of the saints, the contemporary Roman Catholic scholar Leopold Sabourin concludes:

> A close analysis of the evidence presented for the Lourdes miracles and for the miracles of the saints reveals the potential fallibility of human assessments of miracles and the difficulty to ascertain God's direct intervention in extraordinary cures. This does not put into question the opportunity of beatifications or canonizations, since the Pope's pronouncements are not invalidated by mistakes in the verification of the miracles. It does, however, pose the question of the opportunity of requesting miracles almost as *sine qua non* conditions for these solemn acts. It would certainly be better for the church to recognise fewer miracles than to have her judgment tied to dubious ones. But this writer acknowledges that even a modest suggestion in that sense may not be adequately founded on an investigation of so limited proportions. (*The Divine Miracles Discussed and Defended* [Rome: Catholic Book Agency, 1977], p. 172)

It should be added that Sabourin takes note of West's investigations and also reports on other investigations.

Some years ago a major investigation into healing was made in England. It was commissioned by the Church of England, but its scope extended beyond that particular church. The findings were published in *The Church's Ministry of Healing: Report of the Archbishops' Commission* (Westminster, London: The Church Information Office, 1958). The Commission was made up of distinguished members of the church and the medical profession. It collected evidence from a wide variety of sources, including people who at the time were prominent in faith healing and spiritual healing. The

British Medical Association set up a special committee in order to cooperate with the Commission. The B.M.A. report was published separately under the title *Divine Healing and Co-operation between Doctors and Clergy* (London: British Medical Association, 1956). It reached the conclusion that

> We can find no evidence that there is any type of illness cured by "spiritual healing" alone which could not have been cured by medical treatment which necessarily includes consideration of environmental factors. We find that, whilst patients suffering from psychogenic disorders may be "cured" by various methods of spiritual healing, just as they are by methods of suggestion and other forms of psychological treatment employed by doctors, we can find no evidence that organic diseases are cured solely by such means. The evidence suggests that many such cases claimed to be cured are likely to be either instances of wrong diagnosis, wrong prognosis, remission, or possibly of spontaneous cure. (P. 15)

While welcoming the positive benefits that "spiritual ministrations" could bring to patients, the B.M.A. committee expressed reserve concerning the practice of laying on of hands and unction in cases where they could be misunderstood as acting in a magical way (p. 21). The Archbishops' Commission took the point. The sacraments were not to be understood in a shallow, superstitious way. It urged that a sacramental ministry of healing must be preceded by sound sacramental teaching. It also took the opportunity to point out that the church's ministry of healing was not confined to the physical and psychological benefits that it confers. More is involved than making people "quietly cheerful" or giving them a "tonic influence." The ministry of the church is concerned with all that is involved in the "union of God in Christ" (p. 76).

The views of Vincent Edmunds and C. Gordon Scorer in their study *Some Thoughts on Faith Healing* (London: Inter-Varsity Press, 1956, and revised editions) were not markedly different. In their conclusions they noted that while statistics are difficult if not impossible to obtain, there seems to be no appreciable difference in the vital statistics and longevity of those associated with healing and faith movements as compared with the general population. At any rate, they had encountered no claims to the contrary. Edmunds and Scorer ventured to think that in cases of recovery from "malignant growths" the figures for those associated with faith healing appear not to differ much from the rare cases of spontaneous regression in general practice, where no religious influence is claimed. By far the majority of the cures claimed by healing movements are of certain functional conditions, as compared with the *incurable organic*.

In the Introduction I told how in the early days of my ministry I was impressed by Henry Frost's book *Miraculous Healing*. I still am. Frost was not a medical doctor who could speak from the standpoint of professional expertise. Nor was he a theologian in the technical sense of being a trained researcher. But he was a very thoughtful Christian worker and teacher. With a sanctified open mind he examined claims to healing and the teaching of the Scriptures.

Frost was not prepared to say dogmatically that the age of miracles is past and that God never heals in unusual ways today. He examined testimony to unusual healing and testimony to cases where healing was not granted. Some of these cases were relatively trivial, like being cured of a cold and of seasickness. He acknowledged that even in the cases of unusual healing in answer to prayer, the same illnesses returned on other occasions and other ailments were experienced by the same patients.

Frost devoted a substantial part of his book to an examination of the teaching of A. J. Gordon and A. B. Simpson who in their day were the leading advocates of a healing ministry. He considered Gordon's *Ministry of Healing* and Simpson's *Gospel of Healing* to be the best statements available for faith healing. But he also considered the experiences of Gordon and Simpson in the light of their biographies. He concluded: "While no blame is to be attached to these men of God because of their sickness, suffering and death, yet it is a fact that there is a wide discrepancy between their final experiences and what they had taught concerning the Christian's privilege of momentarily and continually deriving physical life from the life of the resurrected Christ" (*Miraculous Healing* [reprint London: Marshall, Morgan and Scott, 1951], p. 54).

I will turn to the theological arguments in a moment. But before I do so two further issues concerning the appeal to experience require comment.

Miracles and Evangelism. The first of these issues has to do with evangelism. It is sometimes argued that traditional Christianity is too cerebral. It addresses the mind, but not the heart. It appeals to reason rather than emotion. This may be all right, it is said, for cultured intellectuals in the Western world. But it makes little headway with Africans, Asians, and Indians. They want a god of power. And if we cannot supply them with a god of power, they will turn back to their traditional gods. The same may be said about the majority of people in the Western world. We have only to look at the papers and magazines near the checkout stands at the supermarkets. What people are interested in are the private lives of royalty, screen and TV personalities, success and power, and miracles of healing. If the Christian church is to make an impact, the argument goes, then it has to meet these needs by offering people a steady diet of big-name personalities and power.

But where does this argument lead? Can the church deliver? Should it deliver? We live in a hurting world. Most people are poor. Sooner or later we all feel deep pain. What can Christianity do about it?

First of all, we must recognize that a Christianity that touches only part of our lives is not a full Christianity. The gospel is concerned with us as whole persons. But this is not to say that the Christian church should set itself up as an agency to meet every human need. No one in his or her right mind would dream up the idea of setting up a church branch of the automobile industry to compete with Ford, General Motors, and the rest. But it is all right for Christians to work in the automobile industry. By doing this they are meeting needs of their fellow human beings.

In the same way, the Christian church has no business setting itself up as an alternative to the medical profession. But Christians have a place in the medical profession. There is no way in which the advocates of faith healing can compete with the combined resources of the medical profession. This is not to say that anyone has a perfect track record. Even with the best professional attention, sooner or later we all die. But if, for the sake of argument, one were to arrange a Mount Carmel type of contest between a team of faith healers and the staff of a local hospital, there is no question about the latter winning out time and time again.

As I see it, the claims of the healers fall into two categories. On the one hand, there are cases where the healer is working in conjunction with treatment provided by the medical profession. In such cases it is not a simple matter of either the prayer or the medical treatment being the cause of the healing. On the other hand, in cases where the healer is working on his own, the successful instances are either minor or trivial. I am thinking of reports of lowered blood pressure, relief of migraine, the easing of minor aches and pains, and the fractional lengthening of legs of people who were unaware of discrepancies in the length of their legs.

If we were to say that the power of our God is revealed in such matters, then we would have to say that his powerlessness is revealed in his failure to relieve the more seriously handicapped. But is this really what the Christian gospel is about? Does it really come down to a power struggle? I do not think so.

But what about other religions? Christianity has no

monopoly on healing, nor even of faith healing. Healings are widely attributed to numerous gods, spirits, and healers. There are testimonies to miracles performed by voodoo spirits in Latin America, Tirupathi Venkateswara in South India, and the Virgin of Guadalupe. The interested reader will find a fund of material in such books as Sudhir Kakar's *Shamans, Mystics and Doctors: A Psychological Inquiry into India and Its Healing Traditions* (Boston: Beacon Press, 1983), and *Magic, Faith and Healing: Studies in Primitive Psychiatry Today*, edited by Ari Kiev, with a foreword by Jerome D. Frank (New York: The Free Press, 1974). Dr. Frank, Professor of Psychiatry at the Johns Hopkins University Medical College, comments:

> The healer, whether psychiatrist or shaman, derives his healing powers from his status and role in the sufferer's society and functions, among other ways, as an evoker of healing forces, a mentor, a role model, and a mediator between the sufferer and his group. His task is to help the patient whether he be a stockbroker, a research scientist, or an African tribesman, to mobilize his psychological and spiritual as well as his bodily resources. (P. xii)

If we think of healing and the Christian gospel simply in terms of power, then we are thinking on the wrong level and in the wrong way. In the last analysis it does not come down to a power struggle between rival gods and rival religions to determine which can do the biggest wonder. The apostle Paul ended his letter to the Philippians with the assurance: "And my God will supply every need of yours according to his riches in glory in Christ Jesus" (Philippians 4:19). Paul knew what he was talking about. He was in prison, on trial for his life. He knew what it was to face plenty and to face hunger, abundance and want. He had learned, in whatever state he was, to be content. Paul had learned to depend on God to judge what his true needs were and how they were to be met. The God who can do that for someone is the God who wins out in the end.

How Do We Interpret Experience? A further point calls for comment before we turn to the theological arguments about healing. It concerns the way we interpret the things we experience. Not every answer to prayer is a sign and wonder. The passing of a migraine, relief from backache, the recovery of peace of mind and a sense of well-being—these are all things for which to be thankful. They are, in the last analysis, gifts from God. But they are like the sunshine and the rain. They come to the just and the unjust. They are not signs and wonders like the events that attended the exodus from Israel or the ministry of Jesus and the apostles.

We cannot therefore take at face value claims that such events are miracles in the sense of manifestations of the direct activity of the Holy Spirit. Likewise we cannot take at face value the claims to supernatural healing that are made in non-Christian circles that are also taken to imply vindication of a particular worldview. Discernment is needed in evaluating *both* Christian and non-Christian claims to healing. In each given instance we need to ask *what* actually happened. We also need to ask *why* it happened. To answer such questions adequately we need to approach them from the standpoints of medicine, anthropology, sociology, psychology, and theology. Only when we do this will we begin to get an adequate answer to our questions.

THE THEOLOGICAL ARGUMENTS

Let us now turn to the New Testament and ask what support it gives to those who claim that the church has a special ministry of healing.

Jesus and Healing. The Gospels tell of two special missions in which Jesus gave his disciples authority to heal and cast out demons. On the first occasion Jesus sent out the Twelve (Matthew 10:1-42; Mark 6:7-13; cf. 3:15; Luke 9:1-6). The second mission is mentioned only in Luke. This time the

Lord sent seventy (some texts read seventy-two) (Luke 10:1-20). But it is clear from the accounts that these were special missions with specific goals and that they came to an end.

When we turn to the Great Commission at the end of Matthew's Gospel, there is no specific mention of healing. The remaining eleven disciples are given the mandate: " 'Go therefore and make disciples of all nations, baptizing them in the name of the Father and of the Son and of the Holy Spirit, teaching them to observe all that I have commanded you; and lo, I am with you always, to the close of the age' " (Matthew 28:19-20). The stress falls on preaching the gospel and on what is involved in being a disciple. Jesus' parting words in Luke and in John make no mention of healing. In John's account the bestowal of the Spirit is linked with the authority to forgive and retain sins (John 20:22-23).

The ending of Mark's Gospel deserves special attention. The original text ends with verse 8 of chapter 16 and the words "for they were afraid." I personally think that that is where Mark intended to end his account, but other people think that Mark's original ending has been lost. At any rate various people in the early church felt that the conclusion in verse 8 was too abrupt, and so they set about supplying an ending that seemed appropriate to them.

The NIV detaches verses 9-20 from the rest of the text and points out that the passage is missing from "the two most reliable early manuscripts." The RSV gives two variant readings, and rightly puts both of them in italics at the bottom of the page, explaining that they are additions found in some manuscripts. They are not contained in the earliest Greek manuscripts of the Gospel. The longer of these endings, however, is given in the Greek text that was used for the KJV translation.

The point to be grasped is that verses 9-20 are not really part of Scripture, and therefore they cannot be credited with the same authority that the rest of the Gospel has. I must add that I make this point not because I have a low view of Scripture, but because I have a high one! It is of the utmost importance to distinguish between what is inspired Scripture and what is not. Verses 9-20 have no more authority as Scripture than (say) the marginal notes and comments found in some study Bibles.

The point has important consequences. It means that we cannot treat as Christ's words the various promises, signs, exorcisms, picking up of poisonous snakes, drinking of poison, or the recovery of the sick on whom the disciples have laid their hands. It would seem that all this was the work of a well-meaning early Christian who felt that it would be appropriate to compose a suitable ending for the Gospel in the light of what he had found in the Acts of the Apostles.

In short, the church has no specific ongoing mandate from Jesus to heal that is recorded in authentic Scripture.

The Experience of the Apostles. When we turn to the accounts of Acts and the various things we can glean from the New Testament letters, we discover that the apostles and others in the church had a gift of healing. Several passages mention signs and wonders (Acts 2:19, 22, 43; 5:12; 6:8; 7:36; 14:3; 15:12). The expression carries with it echoes of the signs and wonders that accompanied God's great saving acts in the Old Testament. The word "sign" is used on its own to describe Peter's healing of the lame man in the temple (Acts 4:16, 22; cf. 3:1-10) and Philip's activity in Samaria (Acts 8:6, 13).

Acts 5:12-16 describes the many healings and exorcisms performed by the apostles and the great response they evoked. Some people even carried their sick out in the streets that Peter's shadow might fall on them as a means of healing. The healings of Peter are counterbalanced by those of Paul, who healed a lame man at Lystra (Acts 14:8), cast out a spirit from a slave girl with a gift for divination at Philippi (Acts 16:16-18), and performed such extraordinary miracles at Ephesus that handerchiefs or aprons were carried from his body for the healing and exorcism of the sick (Acts 19:11-12). At Troas Eutychus survived a fall that everyone except Paul deemed fatal (Acts 20:9-12).

As in the Gospels, the healings and exorcisms produced a mixed reaction. They led to the imprisonment of both Peter and Paul, though both enjoyed miraculous escapes (Acts 5:17-20; 16:19-27). In both cases healing and exorcism provided opportunity to proclaim the word of God (Acts 4:13-22; 5:33-40; 16:31-32). But this did not prevent Paul's later arrest and imprisonment (Acts 21:27-28, 30). Nor did it prevent the gift from being misunderstood. Paul was thought to be a god (Acts 14:11; 28:6). In Samaria Simon Magus judged the Spirit to be a superior form of magic that could be bought (Acts 8:14-24). At Ephesus itinerant Jewish exorcists undertook to practice in the name of Jesus, but failed (Acts 19:11-20). This led to the wholesale abandonment of magic at Ephesus and the opposition of those with vested interests in it.

Paul described his ministry among the Gentiles in terms of winning their obedience "by word and deed, by the power of signs and wonders, by the power of the Holy Spirit" (Romans 15:18-19). He rejected sign-seeking by the Jews and wisdom-seeking by the Gentiles and proclaimed Christ crucified as the power and wisdom of God (1 Corinthians 1:22-25). At the same time he could point to "the demonstration of the Spirit and power" (1 Corinthians 2:4). Healing and miracle working are among the gifts of the Spirit in the body of Christ, but such gifts are given only to some (1 Corinthians 12:28-30). They have their place only in relation to other gifts. Miracle working is a gift of the Spirit that is given to faith (Galatians 3:5). But it is not a fruit of the Spirit, and it exists alongside pain and suffering, as we shall see more fully in the next chapter (Galatians 4:13-15, 19; 5:22-23; 6:8-9, 11, 17).

The experience of the early church presents us with a paradox. Paul could speak of the "signs and wonders and mighty works" that he wrought among the Corinthians "in all patience." He could speak of them as "the signs of a true apostle" (2 Corinthians 12:12). But many of his readers evidently found it hard to reconcile this with the weakness, sickness, and misfortunes that befell him and that he describes in 2 Corinthians 11 and 12. Could he really be an apostle and still be afflicted like that?

The account Paul presents here of his experience (to which may be added the picture that we get from Acts and letters like Philippians) clearly gives the lie to the belief that the Christian life is one continuous success story. Things did not come easily for Paul, or the other apostles and their co-workers for that matter. Sometimes the suggestion is made that there are two kinds of hardship and affliction. There is the hardship and affliction that comes from outside. Over this we have no immediate control. To this category, it is said, belong the imprisonments, opposition, and persecution that Paul suffered. On the other hand, there are physical ailments. It is sometimes suggested that the true man or woman of faith will not be afflicted by these since it is God's will that the wholeness that belongs to salvation excludes this kind of suffering. Moreover, it is said, when Paul talked about his "weakness" (2 Corinthians 10:10; 11:30; 12:9-10) he was not talking about physical ailments, but about things that he suffered for Christ's sake.

Now we can draw a broad distinction between the ills that come to us through external circumstances and the ills that come through physical infirmity. But the above explanation has the air of a theory contrived to fit unwelcome facts. Paul's physical infirmities cannot be excluded from what he says about his weakness. It is true that the Greek word *astheneia* means weakness generally. But its primary, literal meaning is weakness that includes sickness and disease. This sense cannot be excluded from the meaning of a passage unless there is indication in the passage to the contrary. The same applies to the verb *astheneō* (be sick, weak) and the adjective *asthenēs* (weak, feeble, sick).

A case in point is the letter of James. Toward the end of the letter James asks, "Is any among you sick?" (James 5:14). The verb here is *asthenei*. No one would translate this as, "Is any among you weak?" The passage clearly refers to the sick in the Christian community. We shall return to the question of living with sickness in the final chapter, where we shall see that not even the apostle Paul was exempt from sickness and that sometimes it is God's will that we have to live with our sickness and triumph in spite of it. In the meantime, it is worth noting that miraculous healing was by no means the norm in the New Testament. Epaphroditus was ill, near to death (Philippians 2:27). Trophimus had to be left behind at Miletus on account of his illness (2 Timothy 4:20). Paul had his thorn in the flesh (2 Corinthians 12:7). Natural remedies were recommended. Paul urged Timothy, "No longer drink only water, but use a little wine for the sake of your stomach and your frequent ailments" (1 Timothy 5:23).

The Anointing of the Sick in James. There has been a great deal of discussion concerning the recommendations in James 5:13-16.

> Is any one among you suffering? Let him pray. Is any cheerful? Let him sing praise. Is any among you sick? Let him call for the elders of the church, and let them pray over him, anointing him with oil in the name of the Lord; and the prayer of faith will save the sick man, and the Lord will raise him up; and if he has committed sins, he will be forgiven. Therefore confess your sins to one another, and pray for one another, that you may be healed. The prayer of a righteous man has great power in its effects.

Apart from Mark 6:13, this is the only instance in the New Testament of anointing with oil. It is the only passage where this procedure is recommended or even referred to.

The early church came to see in this passage the ground for the practice of anointing the dying. From the Reformation onward people have seen in it recommendations for prayer for the sick. After all, the passage speaks of the Lord raising up the sick, and it mentions healing in response to prayer. More recently, the passage is seen as supplying the justification for services of anointing and healing.

The more I look at this passage the more I think that we should not be too hasty in dismissing the interpretation of the early church. Clearly, James is not recommending healing services as they are sometimes held today. For one thing, the passage does not apply to everyone. It applies to those "among you," i.e., within the Christian community, who are sick. The practice is not recommended as an evangelistic tool. Nor is it offered to outsiders. Moreover, it is not a case of bringing the sick to church or to a meeting. Rather, the elders are to come to the sick person. This suggests to me that the person is too sick to come to the regular meetings of the church.

There is no suggestion that the elders have a special gift of healing, or perhaps that someone in the church has such a gift. The rite is one of reconciliation involving the elders of the church, as those responsible for discipline and pastoral care, and the confession of sins. There is an ambiguity about James's language. On one level, it looks as if James is talking about physical healing and reminding his readers that God does indeed answer prayer for healing, just as he answered Elijah's prayer for rain. But there is a deeper level of meaning underlying his words. The verbs "save" and "raise up" can be used of healing and raising from the sickbed. But they are also used of salvation from sin and eternal death and the resurrection to eternal life. The word "heal" is used of restoration to health. But it can also mean healing from sin.

In the context of the argument of the letter of James as a whole, the passage may be seen as a word of comfort to the dying. The letter spends a great deal of time and energy condemning shallow Christianity. It condemns the unbridled tongue, the religion of the rich that cares nothing for the poor, the religion that makes a great deal of faith but produces no works, the religion of the self-seeking. But at the end, having removed all ground for complacency and self-satisfaction, James gives a word of hope. Sickness is not to be taken as God's final word of judgment, as many Jews believed (cf. Job 3:7-9; John 9:2). God answers the prayer of faith of those who are reconciled to their brethren in the church and have received anointing as the sign of their consecration. God will raise them up, forgive them their sins, and grant them the ultimate healing.

Healing and the Incarnation. In support of the gospel of health and healing it is sometimes argued that we should expect health and healing in the light of the incarnation and the atonement and in view of the greater privileges that the Christian has as a member of the new covenant. Several factors are involved here, and we need to examine them in turn.

What truth is there in the claim that we should expect the gifts of health and healing in view of the incarnation? Paul taught that the church was the body of Christ (Romans 12; 1 Corinthians 12; Ephesians 4:16; Colossians 1:18). Clearly this cannot mean that Christians are exempt from hardship. The servant is not greater than his Lord (John 13:16). Like his master, he is called to serve (Mark 10:43-45). He is to count the cost and take up his cross (Luke 14:26-35).

Paul's understanding of the church as the body of Christ does not mean that everyone has the same gift. And the gifts of healing and working miracles are mentioned as gifts of the Spirit only in 1 Corinthians 12:9-10. Here they receive passing mention alongside other gifts. Similarly, the working of miracles receives passing mention in Galatians 3:5. But these are not gifts to the church as a whole. Nor do they receive much prominence in Paul's letters.

It is simply a misuse of Scripture to take a passage like Luke 4:18-19 (which applies to Jesus) or 2 Corinthians 12:12 (which applies to Paul as an apostle) and say that they apply to everyone in the church. In other words, there is nothing to suggest that because Jesus and Paul did miracles, the same gift is passed on to all members of the church.

The Promise Concerning Greater Works. What then about the promise, " 'Truly, truly, I say to you, he who believes in me will also do the works that I do; and greater works than these will he do, because I go to the Father. Whatever you ask in my name, I will do it, that the Father may be glorified in the Son; if you ask anything in my name, I will do it' " (John 14:12-14)? Does this mean that we should all expect to be able to do miracles? Does it mean that we are falling short as believers if we don't do signs and wonders?

Like so many other statements in John, this statement has a certain cryptic quality about it. Think, for example, about the statements on the need to be born again, on Jesus as the bread that came down from heaven, and on the true vine, and about the statement that has just preceded the present one to the effect that he who has seen Jesus has seen the Father. These statements are not literally but figuratively true!

In the literal, physical sense the disciples did not do greater works than Jesus. They did not change water into wine, feed five thousand people, or walk on water. Although they did some astonishing things, not even the raising of Dorcas (Acts 9:36-43) was as striking as the raising of Lazarus, who had been in the tomb four days. The Acts of the Apostles tells of various healings, but they were not on the same scale as those performed by Jesus, and they appear to have been more sporadic.

On the other hand, the ministry of the apostles extended beyond the geographic limits of Jesus' ministry. They won more people to faith. Moreover, the "work of God" is described in John 6:28-29 as believing in him whom God has sent.

John 5:20 also speaks of "greater works." The context explains these words in terms of the Son giving life to the dead and granting eternal life to those who believe. Likewise, the "greater things" mentioned in John 1:50 refer to the revelation of Jesus as the mediator.

If we follow through the thought of John 14:12 as it is worked out in the remainder of the Gospel, we see that the disciples are given the promise and mandate to bear fruit (John 15:16), which again is linked with an invitation to ask the Father in Jesus' name. The disciples are promised the Paraclete who will convict the world of sin, righteousness, and judgment (John 16:7-11). Finally, the disciples are given the Holy Spirit and with him the authority to forgive and retain sins (John 20:22-23).

In other words, neither the context of John nor the information we have from elsewhere in the New Testament supports the interpretation of this passage as a promise to do greater physical miracles. Physical miracles are in fact lesser works when compared with those that have to do with the conviction of sin and forgiveness, judgment, salvation, and eternal life.

Faith That Moves Mountains. The same must be said about the promise concerning the mountain being cast into the sea (Matthew 21:20-22; Mark 11:20-24). In the context nothing is said about miracles of healing. The saying is prompted by the disciples' wonder at the withering of the fig tree that Jesus had cursed. The language recalls several Old Testament themes.

Isaiah 2, Micah 4, and other passages speak of the mountain of the LORD. Zechariah 14:4 speaks of the splitting of the Mount of Olives when the day of the Lord comes. Psalm 2:6 speaks of setting God's king on Zion, his holy hill. Psalm 46:2 declares: "Therefore we will not fear though the earth should change, though the mountains shake in the heart of the sea." If the mountain in the saying refers to Mount Zion, the saying is a promise that marks the end of the Old Testament order that centered on Jerusalem as the mountain of the LORD. It is a word of encouragement not to fear though the old order is collapsing. It is a bestowal of authority to renounce the old order. As such it follows on the cursing of the fig tree, which was a symbolic act of judgment on the failure of Judaism to bring forth the fruit of response to the coming of Christ.

But there may also be a deeper meaning. In Mark's account the saying leads directly to the saying concerning the forgiveness of sins: " 'And whenever you stand praying, forgive, if you have anything against any one; so that your Father also who is in heaven may forgive you your trespasses' " (Mark 11:25). At the end of the book of the prophet Micah there is the saying: "He will again have compassion upon us, he will tread our iniquities under foot. Thou wilt cast all our sins into the depths of the sea" (Micah 7:19). There is no greater blessing for human beings than forgiveness. The removal of the mountain of sin is possible only through the prayer of faith.

Healing and the Atonement. Two further arguments are sometimes used on behalf of a "gospel" of health and healing for all. The first has to do with Matthew's use of Isaiah 53:4: "This was to fulfil what was spoken by the prophet Isaiah, 'He took our infirmities and bore our diseases' " (Matthew 8:17). From this it is argued that there is healing in the atonement and that henceforth believers can and should expect to live a healthy life. But the argument claims too much. Matthew certainly sees a fulfilment of the prophecy in the healings and exorcisms of Jesus, but neither here nor in 1 Peter 2:24 which quotes Isaiah 53:5 is physical healing actually said to be in the atoning death of Christ. Matthew's use of the passage in Isaiah goes on further to say that Jesus' earthly ministry in healing the sick was a fulfilment of that part of Isaiah's servant prophecy which speaks of his bearing our sickness and pains. But even if we say that the atonement is the ground of our victory over all our ills and enemies, it does not follow that we experience the full fruits of them here and now.

Salvation and Wholeness. The other argument is the rather general one that claims that salvation involves wholeness and that the privileges and promises of the new covenant must be greater than those of the old covenant. The argument is further bound up with the apparently open-ended invitations to pray in faith expecting an answer. My response is along the following lines.

First, we need to see that the open-ended invitations to ask in prayer are not quite so open-ended as some people make out. God does indeed honor faith (Matthew 9:29; Hebrews 11:6; James 1:6-8). But it has to be faith *in him,* and prayer has to be *in his name.* Satan promises all manner of things that he cannot deliver. The believer is to live not by bread alone but by every word that proceeds out of the mouth of God (Matthew 4:4; Luke 4:4; Deuteronomy 8:3). We cannot truly pray for anything *in his name* if it is out of character with God's revealed will and promises. As we saw just now in looking at John 14:12, Matthew 21:20-22, and Mark 11:20-24, these promises are not open-ended invitations to ask for material wealth or physical well-being. God's greatest promises have to do with the forgiveness of sins and the gift of eternal life.

Secondly, we must recognize that alongside those who are blessed with goods, wealth, and long life are those saints of God who are not so blessed. In the Old Testament the figure of Job stands as a constant reminder that hardship and suffering can come especially to the godly. The so-called "comforters" of Job who attributed his suffering to his sin and lack of godliness are the ones who receive the book's condemnation. The beatitudes of Jesus say nothing about material wealth or health (Matthew 5:1-12; Luke 6:20-23), though they have much to say about present hardship and the cost of discipleship. The woes recorded by Luke condemn the wealthy and the self-satisfied.

We have already seen how the apostle Paul spoke of his "weaknesses." His life was a living testimony to the truth that God's grace is sufficient and that his power is made perfect in weakness (2 Corinthians 12:9). When judged by the standards of material success and well-being Paul's life was a monumental calamity. Outwardly he was much better off before his conversion than after it. From then on Paul went from one trial to another. If he had to boast, he protested, he would boast of the things that showed his weakness (2 Corinthians 11:30). The only way we can get a gospel of sunny success out of the New Testament is to cut out Paul and his writings, ignore the trials that befell so many others, and remove the cross.

Thirdly, we need to recognize that there are distinctions between what God has covenanted to do and what he has not covenanted to do, between what God may do and what he has promised to do. God is the healer (Exodus 15:26) and the one who is behind all healing. But in the Old Testament health and healing were not automatically guaranteed by membership in the covenant. Miraculous healing figures very little in the Old Testament. The promise to the Israelites of being spared the diseases that afflicted the Egyptians was linked with the obligation to separate themselves from the surrounding peoples and observe strictly the hygienic, dietary, and other laws that were laid upon them (Deuteronomy 7:12-15). Observance of these laws was the means by which the Israelites avoided the diseases that afflicted the surrounding nations.

The new covenant does not promise healing for all now. It promises forgiveness of sins (Matthew 26:28). There is no specific, unqualified promise of health and healing in the New Testament to those who have faith. But there are promises of forgiveness and grace to those who repent and believe (e.g., Matthew 11:28; John 1:12; 3:16-18; Acts 2:38-39; 16:31; 17:30). The church is given authority to pronounce the forgiveness of sins in the name of Christ and the authority of the Spirit (John 20:23; cf. Matthew 18:15-20). But it has no parallel authority to heal. If God heals, it is an uncovenanted mercy. But when he forgives, it is a covenanted mercy.

Fourthly and finally, the claim to health and healing as part of the wholeness that belongs to salvation is like the claims to spiritual perfection that have been made from time to time in the history of the church. The Bible does not have a single conception of salvation, wholeness, and peace (or Shalom) that embraces peace, prosperity, health, and sanctification as *present* realities to be enjoyed by all believers.

In this life, as a sheer matter of fact we do not enjoy complete freedom from sin. We are not spared the trials, the tribulations, and the striving that belong to this world. Paul knew what it was to experience the conflict between the Spirit and the flesh (Galatians 5:16-25). The experiences he describes in Romans 7 and 8 are the experiences he knew as a Christian. He describes them in the present tense. He knows full well that the creation is subject to futility. It is groaning in travail. It belongs to the *future* hope that the creation itself "will be set free from its bondage to decay and obtain the glorious liberty of the children of God" (Romans 8:21).

DANGERS OF EXPECTING COVENANTED HEALING

There is, however, another side to the simplistic assumptions that salvation is the same as wholeness and that God has covenanted to heal everyone who turns to him in faith. It has to do with the burdens that we put on ourselves and on others once we make these assumptions.

People who need healing are already under stress. If prayer for healing is not answered, the stress is intensified by the guilt they feel about their lack of faith. The original pain and suffering can be worsened by the ensuing mental and spiritual turmoil. It is made worse still if the sufferer is surrounded by well-meaning friends who—like Job's comforters—say that the reason for lack of healing is some unconfessed sin or failure really to trust in God. But how much faith do we really need to have in order to be healed? This is a question people sometimes ask, but I do not think the Bible thinks in this way. It is not the amount of faith that matters but where it is placed. Jesus spoke of faith as a minuscule mustard seed (Matthew 17:20; Luke 17:6). Faith is trusting God to do what he has promised. And with this we are brought back to the question of what God has really covenanted to do.

Many bereaved people are prone to depression and guilt because of the nagging feeling that they did not love enough or care enough for the one whom they have now lost. If the bereaved are taught that God has covenanted to heal those who are prayed for in faith, this depression and guilt can be intensified. It can make them feel that they are personally responsible for the death of their loved one because they did not pray enough or believe enough. Instead of finding comfort and hope in the assurances of God's gift of eternal life to those who turn to him, such people can be subjected to the Satanic temptation to self-recrimination and despair.

In cases of depression and the feeling of utter worthlessness the doctrine of covenanted healing can actually have the reverse of its intended effect. For it can actually intensify the original stress and cause sufferers to be even more depressed. The last thing they need is more depression over why the depression has not gone away simply by praying about it. What they need is to be reassured of their heavenly Father's love, whose grace is sufficient at all times.

There are cases where continual striving for healing may actually prevent healing. In her book *Beyond Ourselves* (New York: McGraw-Hill, 1961) Catherine Marshall talks about "the prayer of relinquishment." An illness had kept her in bed for many months. A bevy of specialists seemed unable to help. To quote her own words, "Persistent prayer, using all the faith that I could muster, had resulted in—nothing." Then one afternoon she read a pamphlet by a missionary who had been an invalid for eight years. Worn out by futile petition, the missionary had prayed:

> "All right. I give up. If You want me to be an invalid for the rest of my days, that's Your business. Anyway, I've discovered that I want You even more than I want health. You decide." (P. 83)

Within two weeks the missionary was out of bed and healed. Although it made no sense to her, Catherine Marshall prayed a similar prayer. She did not have faith as she understood faith. She expected nothing. But the result was "as if windows had opened in heaven." From that moment recovery began.

One special danger that may come if we assume that God has covenanted to heal everyone if only he or she has enough faith is the danger that we make faith a substitute for proper care and medical attention. Hardly a month passes that the news media do not give a report of some tragic case in which someone has made the mistake of assuming that faith was an adequate alternative to proper medical care. The sincerity of those who make this mistake is not in question. What must be questioned is the folly of thinking that faith requires us to abandon the means God has provided for the well-being of humankind.

Perfect health and healing are not things that we have any right to expect just because we are Christians. They are not guaranteed to us as our birthright any more than total and instantaneous sanctification. Nor has anyone the right to hold out promises of them to people if only they will believe. The real situation is more like that envisaged in the prayer composed in 1934 by Reinhold Niebuhr that has since been adopted by Alcoholics Anonymous and other bodies.

> O God, give us
> >Serenity to accept what cannot be changed,
> >Courage to change what should be changed,
> >And wisdom to distinguish the one from the other.

13 / "My Grace Is Sufficient"

But he said to me, "My grace is sufficient for you, for my power is made perfect in weakness." (2 Corinthians 12:9)

TWO CASE HISTORIES

I began the previous chapter with a quotation from George. George is a friend of mine. We were driving along the freeway between Los Angeles and San Diego on the way to a meeting. I have known George for some years now. I know him as a respected colleague and friend. He and his wife are among those people who truly radiate Christ and the joy of the Lord. George and his wife were missionaries for many years. He has a Ph.D. in New Testament studies. Though now in so-called retirement, he is more active than most of us in our prime.

George has also had cancer, and not only cancer but an ailment that threatened the loss of sight in one eye. As we were driving along, he said to me, "We must not box God in." In a way, this says it all. God is the healer behind all healing. But there is no foolproof technique for getting a handle on God. No two cases are identical.

David Watson was a Christian minister in England who was much used by God. He enjoyed a worldwide ministry and was loved by thousands. In his prime he was diagnosed as having cancer of the liver. He was operated on and received medical treatment. A pastor friend whose ministry was associated with healing flew from California to London together with two colleagues in order to pray over him. David

Watson tells his story in his book *Fear No Evil: One Man Deals with Terminal Illness* (Wheaton: Harold Shaw Publishers, 1985). One of them laid his hands on David's abdomen. The three colleagues continued to pray, cursing the cancer in the name of Christ and commanding it to wither, and then they claimed God's healing in David's body.

Just over a year after receiving the fatal diagnosis David Watson died. *Fear No Evil* can be read as an account of how physical healing did not come—despite all the expert medical attention, the prayers of countless people, the cursing of the cancer, the words of prophecy, and the claims to healing. But it can also be read as a testimony to something greater—a testimony as to how a saint of God coped with the fears that we all have, how he faced dying and became ready to "go home." A month before he died David Watson preached his last sermon. It was on Psalm 91.

> He who dwells in the shelter of the Most High,
> Who abides in the shadow of the Almighty,
> Will say to the LORD, "My refuge and my fortress;
> My God, in whom I trust."

My friend George went into the hospital and was operated on. People prayed. He recovered from cancer. But they could not operate on his eye. The operation was too delicate. It was not worth the risk. But George was advised by a nutritionist to keep to a strict diet. Within a period of three months his eye trouble cleared up. As we talked about his illness and his healing, George said to me, "You know, it is just crazy to expect God to heal if we don't take care of our bodies and what we eat." This was not meant in any way as a judgment on people who get sick. It was more a warning, as when Paul asked, "Are we to continue in sin that grace may abound?" (Romans 6:1). Can we really expect God to step in to do miracles for us when we are not willing to do the things that are needed to look after ourselves?

WHAT CAN WE EXPECT OF GOD?

What can we expect of God? What is the Bible saying to us today on the subject of healing?

Miracles No Guarantee of Godliness. The New Testament describes how Jesus healed people and cast out demons. It also describes incidents that depict him as having supernatural power over nature—power that belongs to God himself. The apostles and others were given gifts of healing and authority to cast out demons. But, as we saw in the previous chapter, the gifts mentioned in the Gospels were linked with the specific mission of the Twelve and the Seventy to prepare the way for Jesus. It is a sobering thought that Judas Iscariot was among the disciples who received these gifts. It is also sobering to recall the warning given in the Sermon on the Mount: " 'On that day many will say to me, "Lord, Lord, did we not prophesy in your name, and cast out demons in your name, and do many mighty works in your name?" And then will I declare to them, "I never knew you; depart from me, you evildoers" ' " (Matthew 7:22-23). Gifts of healing and exorcism are not in themselves guarantees of godliness—not even when associated with the name of the Lord. From the early centuries onward the name of Jesus has been used in magic. The Hindu Subba Rao and many others use the name of Jesus to heal and cast out demons. Voodoo priests do the same. It is not surprising that the New Testament contains many warnings against false prophets and false signs (Matthew 24:24; Mark 13:22; Colossians 2:8; 1 Timothy 4:1-2; 2 Timothy 4:3) and that it urges believers to test the spirits lest they be led astray (1 John 4:1; 2:26).

Ongoing Miracles? What are we to make of all this? My reflections on experience and my study of the New Testament suggest to me that the miracles that we read about in the New Testament were bound up with the manifestation of

Jesus as the Son of God and his decisive work in salvation history. But they are not typical ongoing events. The signs and wonders belong to God's special saving acts, but they are not everyday occurrences. There is no specific mention of healing in the ongoing mandate of Christ to the church. There is no unqualified promise of physical health and healing to those who believe, any more than there is an unqualified promise of wealth and prosperity.

This is not to say that there are no gifts of healing today inside the church—or outside it, for that matter. But in the discussion of gifts of the Spirit, as in Romans 12, 1 Corinthians 12, and Ephesians 4, it is clear that not everyone has the same gift. Healing and miracles are mentioned in these lists only in 1 Corinthians 12:9-10, 28-30, and then only in passing. They have their place in the total ministry alongside other gifts and ministries. As we saw in the previous chapter, physical healing is not the greatest or the most important gift of God. The healing of the body is of much less importance than the healing of the soul. God's greatest gifts are the forgiveness of sins, peace with God, and eternal life.

In the New Testament wholeness may have to be sacrificed for the sake of salvation. The Sermon on the Mount contains the warning: " 'If your right eye causes you to sin, pluck it out and throw it away; it is better that you lose one of your members than that your whole body be thrown into hell. And if your right hand causes you to sin, cut it off and throw it away; it is better that you lose one of your members than that your whole body go into hell' " (Matthew 5:29-30; cf. Mark 9:43-47).

This is not to say that one should not pray for healing. Nor is it to say that one may pray for anything but healing! In the previous chapter we noted numerous encouragements to pray and to trust God. They could be summed up in the exhortation that Paul wrote from prison to the Philippians: "Have no anxiety about anything, but in everything by prayer and supplication with thanksgiving let your requests be made known to God. And the peace of God, which passes all understanding, will keep your hearts and your minds in Christ Jesus" (Philippians 4:6-7).

Healing and Faith. But we cannot go on to draw the conclusion that only our lack of faith prevents us from being healed. Few things are more cruel than to say to someone who is crippled with pain or terminally ill that it is only his or her lack of faith that prevents healing. Lack of faith may well be an impediment to us sometimes. Failure to pray may well be a reason why we do not enjoy the peace of God and the gifts of God. But they are not necessarily the cause of our suffering. The reasons may lie elsewhere.

Paul encouraged the Philippian Christians to pray. But he went on to say that he had learned, in whatever state he was, to be content. He knew how to be abased, and he knew how to abound. He could face plenty, and he could face want. He could handle all things in Christ who gave him strength (Philippians 4:13). This included what he had earlier described—his imprisonment and uncertainty whether he would live or die (Philippians 1:17-26).

It is not necessarily an admission of our lack of faith if we add to our prayers the qualification, ". . . if it is thy will." To say this is not necessarily an admission of doubt—though it may be. Even the apostle Paul confessed that we do not know what to pray for as we ought (Romans 8:26). We need the Spirit to intercede for us according to the will of God. In the Garden of Gethsemane Jesus himself prayed, " 'Abba, Father, all things are possible to thee; remove this cup from me; yet not what I will, but what thou wilt' " (Mark 14:36; cf. Matthew 26:39, 42; Luke 22:42). If we make such prayers our own, we are not confessing doubt in the power of God, but our human ignorance in knowing what is best for us. It is not a confession of doubt, but the highest confession of faith and trust, to pray the words of the Lord's Prayer, " 'Thy will be done' " (Matthew 6:10).

I think it was H. L. Mencken who observed that for every complex problem there was always a simple solution—which was almost invariably wrong. The same could be said about sickness and healing. The simplistic solutions of the extremists are attractive precisely because they are simple. But it is as wrong to say that the Christian church has no part at all in the ministry of healing as it is to say that the only thing that prevents people from being healed is lack of faith.

It is simplistic and dangerous to take biblical texts out of context and use them as pretexts for justifying our practices. The signs, wonders, and miracles mentioned in Hebrews 2:4 belong to the witness that God gave to the saving work of Christ, but the passage contains no suggestion that they will continue for all time. The "signs of a true apostle" (2 Corinthians 12:12) are signs that distinguish an apostle from other people! The fact that Paul performed such signs does not mean that we should be able to do the same. It is wrongheaded to take prophecies like Isaiah 42:1-3 and 61:1-2, which applied specifically to Jesus, and to apply them to ourselves and our ministries.

Healing and Demonology. It is equally wrongheaded to attribute all sickness to demonic powers and to treat healing as if it were basically a matter of exorcism. As we saw earlier, the Gospel accounts draw a clear distinction between healing on the one hand and the casting out of demons on the other. The two are not identical, and Jesus did not treat them in the same way. In cases where the root of the trouble was personal—such as the need of forgiveness, the need of God's creative and redemptive word, psychological need, or demonic possession—Jesus addressed the problem with his word. Where the trouble was physical, Jesus healed by his touch or through some physical act. Where the trouble was a combination of these sets of factors (e.g., the possessed epileptic boy in Mark 9), Jesus used a combination of word and touch. Jesus did not touch the possessed while the demons were still in possession. He touched the boy in Mark 9 only *after* the unclean spirit had come out of him.

What is striking in all this is the marked difference between Jesus and some modern-day beliefs and practices. Nothing in the New Testament suggests that all physical illness is attributable to demonic activity. Possession is attributed to demons, but other illnesses are not. The case of the woman whom Satan had bound for eighteen years (Luke 13:16) is no exception. The affliction was ultimately attributable to Satan, but the case was not one of demon possession. Jesus did not treat the woman as he treated cases of possession and exorcism.

There is no suggestion in the New Testament or anywhere in the Bible that different parts of the human body are subject to different demons. Nor are we given any encouragement to develop an interest in the demonic in order to pursue a ministry of healing or any other ministry.

Again, we do not find any warrant in the New Testament for cursing particular diseases. This was not the practice of Jesus. He did not curse the blindness of the blind or the leprosy of the lepers. He did not even curse the demons. He rebuked them and commanded them to be silent and to pass out of those who were possessed. The only instance of Jesus cursing anything is that of the fig tree. This was not part of his healing ministry, but a symbolic act of judgment on the people's failure to produce fruit at the day of the Lord. Cursing in Jesus' teaching belongs to the last judgment (Matthew 25:41).

For the reasons that I gave in the last chapter, I do not think that mental illness is the same as demon possession or that demon possession is the same as mental illness. Possession, however, may make a person mentally ill. The unqualified are not to undertake ministry either to the possessed or to the mentally ill.

The New Testament contains clear warnings about demonic transference (Matthew 8:31-32; 12:43-45; Mark 5:12-13). In *But Deliver Us From Evil* (London: Darton, Longman and Todd, 1974, pp. 142-43) John Richards records a story told by Christopher Woodard in *A Doctor's Faith Holds Fast*. A young soldier went out of his mind as a result of the strain he had gone through. He became very violent. The army doctor examined him and was reminded of the story in the New Testament about the man on the shore of the lake. He called in the chaplain while the young soldier was held down by half a dozen others. The chaplain was taken aback. But not wishing to appear nonplussed, he said, "In the name of Jesus Christ I command this thing to come out of you!" So saying, he made the sign of the cross. The boy appeared to return to normal, but the chaplain dropped dead.

The experience of the church with the demonic makes it imperative that only those with proper experience and authority, using the appropriate forms mandated by the church, undertake such a ministry. The Roman Catholic Church has clear rubrics on exorcism that are to be followed precisely. The report of the Exeter Commission in the Anglican Church made very specific recommendations concerning the practice of exorcism. Exorcism is not part of the pastoral duties of the ordinary minister. It should be undertaken only by exorcists authorized by the bishop, and then only with proper preparation, using the prescribed forms and in cooperation with a medical doctor and a doctor of psychiatry.

It would be folly to ignore the warnings and recommendations of those who have long experience in these matters. It would equally be folly for well-intentioned Christians to treat cases of mental illness as if they were spiritual problems. Here again wisdom is needed to distinguish one from the other. It requires both discernment and humility on the part of the pastor or minister to distinguish a case of mental illness from a spiritual problem and to refer the patient to the appropriate therapist. The converse is also true. Many of the problems that afflict people today are at bottom spiritual problems and demand a spiritual solution.

To say all this is simply to give recognition to the fact that as creatures in a created world we have different needs. Moreover, the created order is such that God has provided appropriate but different ways for those needs to be met. To speak in this way is, of course, to speak from the standpoint of Christian faith. I make no apology for this. For I am trying to look at life from the standpoint of the Christian faith. But faith is not a shortcut to solving problems. Faith is not an alternative to work. It is not an alternative to following the paths that God has decreed, or to availing ourselves of the things that God has provided for the use and well-being of his creatures. In other words, we do not expect crops to grow without being tended. We do not expect buildings to be built just by praying for them. Neither should we expect health and healing to come without due care for our minds and bodies and without availing ourselves of the vast resources of medical knowledge, skill, and care that exist in the world.

A Secularized Worldview? If this sounds like a semisecularized view of the world to some, my answer is that it is implicit in the biblical view of creation. The Old Testament stories of creation deliberately exclude the demonic element from their accounts. Creation comes about through the Word of God. The created world is not a compound of the divine and the demonic. Genesis 1 does not mention the sun and the moon as such. They are not astral bodies exerting some kind of mysterious spiritual influence. They are just lights! They are there to give light by day and by night and to mark off the days and the season. They do not exert astral influences on the earth. They are not quasi-deities. It belongs to the creation mandate to treat the creation as creation. From its very first chapter the Bible itself "secularizes" the world order in the sense that it insists that things should be treated for what they are in themselves within the total structure of God's created order.

This kind of "secularization" finds expression in the theistic monotheism that runs throughout Scripture. The demonic is absolutely excluded from Old Testament religion. Satan and the demonic have been decisively defeated and overcome by Christ (see, e.g., Matthew 12:27-29; Mark 3:24-27; Luke 10:18; 11:17-22; John 12:31; Colossians 1:13; 2:15). We do not have to repeat the work of Christ. It is an accomplished fact.

This in itself means that things can have their proper place in life. We do not have to resort to the supernatural in place of the natural. The natural remedies that the Good Samaritan used on the man by the wayside (Luke 10:34) and that which Paul urged Timothy to take (1 Timothy 5:23) were the right remedies in the situation. When Luke became a Christian he did not cease to be a physician. Paul does not speak of him as "the ex-physician." He calls him "the beloved physician" (Colossians 4:14). In view of the "weaknesses" that Paul had, Luke doubtless cared for Paul not only as a Christian companion but also by drawing on his professional skill.

When we turn to God in prayer, we are not seeking an alternative route to the one God has normally provided. Prayer is not that kind of shortcut. Prayer is an activity in which we seek to bring ourselves into line with the will of God and at the same time share our concerns with him and be in fellowship with him. It does not relieve us from doing our part. But it is an acknowledgment that God also has a part to play in our affairs. It is an expression of our readiness to let God be God and the God of our lives.

When Christians pray "in the name of Jesus Christ," they are not using his name as a magical formula. This is not to say that it has never been used as a magical formula and that it could not be so used today. There are plenty of magical texts in existence in which the name of Jesus is used. From the earliest days of the church there are instances of trying to treat Christianity as a form of magic. Acts 8:9-26 tells of Simon Magus who believed and was baptized, and who evidently thought of the Spirit as a form of superior magic. Acts 19:13-16 tells of Jewish exorcists who "undertook to pronounce the name of the Lord Jesus over those who had evil spirits." The attempt met with disastrous consequences.

It is not as if there is power in the name that is released by use of the name when uttered in the right way in connection with the correct formula. The Christian use of the name of the Lord Jesus Christ is an expression of the Christian's personal commitment. It is a confession of faith and the acknowledgment that it is because of him that the believer presumes to approach the Father. It is a public declaration of the grounds on which the believer presumes to act.

The Place of Healing and Exorcism. Nowhere in the New Testament is the ministry of healing and exorcism regarded simply as a tool of evangelism. In Jesus' own ministry it belonged to the baptism of the Holy Spirit—the cleansing, renewing, consecrating work of Jesus in the power of the Spirit as he summoned men and women to enter the Kingdom of God. It was not designed to soften people up for accepting his message. It was not a kind of bargaining chip that he used to entice people. Rather, it was the expression of his loving compassion. As such it had its place alongside his other acts of caring, compassion, and renewal. It was the embodiment of his teaching in action.

In the same way, where the church has a ministry of caring and prayer for healing today, the focus should not be on the sensational. It should not be a kind of advertisement to pull people in. It should not center on the minister or the evangelist as a cult figure. It should be done in the name of Christ in order to meet the needs of the needy.

THE HEALING OF THE SPIRIT

There is a healing ministry of the Christian church that is not necessarily a "gift" in the special sense of the term. It is not a "gift" in the sense of being able to do things that the medical profession cannot do by producing wonder cures. It is a ministry of caring and concern. As such it may accompany the ministry of the medical profession; it is concerned with the wholeness of people, but reckons with the fact that we do not always get wholeness in this life. It is a ministry to those who recognize (or perhaps still need to recognize) that we are not always the kind of persons that we would like to be. Life has not always treated us the way we would like to be treated. We have not been given all the things that our self-esteem tells us is our due. Most of us have to enter into life hurt or maimed in one way or another.

The ministry I am talking about concerns the things that Dennis and Matthew Linn are talking about in their book *Healing Life's Hurts* (New York: Paulist Press, 1978). It is the ministry of inner healing—the healing of the human spirit. It has to do with acceptance—accepting others and being accepted, accepting ourselves and accepting God. It has to do with the healing of memories—our denial of what is there, our anger, our deep-down determination to try to bargain our way out, our depression, our endeavor to avoid the way of acceptance. This ministry is the ministry of reconciliation—reconciliation with God, with ourselves, and with our fellow human beings.

In some cases the healing of the spirit leads to the healing of the body. In others it does not. Many of the most renowned figures in the history of the church were plagued by ill health or died young. The names of Martin Luther, John Calvin, Robert Murray McCheyne, C. H. Spurgeon, Fanny Crosby, and Frances Ridley Havergal spring readily to mind. The apostle Paul spoke of his thorn in the flesh. The subject is of real importance because it throws light on the problem of pain and suffering.

Paul's Thorn in the Flesh. Some have suggested that the thorn in the flesh (2 Corinthians 12:7) was a personal enemy. But the suggestion looks more like a last-ditch attempt to avoid the implication that Paul was actually physically sick. Elsewhere personal opponents are mentioned even by name (2 Timothy 2:17; 4:14), but they are not described in these terms. We have no knowledge either from Acts or from Paul's own writings that there was one special opponent who remained with Paul attacking him despite Paul's prayerful entreaties to God.

More plausible are the suggestions that Paul may have used the expression to describe continuing fits of depression, migraine, deafness, and even epilepsy. But these explanations do not really seem to fit Paul's life as we know it from the New Testament. We must acknowledge that any attempt to identify the thorn in the flesh must be speculative and based on circumstantial evidence. But then all attempts at historical explanation involve these factors. My own view is that Paul was referring to his defective eyesight.

The fact that Paul was given the thorn in the flesh to prevent him from being too elated with visions and revelations may itself be indicative that the affliction had something to do with his sight. We know from the accounts of his conversion in Acts 9, 22, and 26 that Paul was temporarily blinded through his encounter with the risen Christ but that his sight was restored. But Paul's failure to recognize the high priest when he was brought before the Sanhedrin may be a further indication that his sight was impaired (Acts 23:1, 5).

The suggestion that Paul was afflicted with ill health is given some weight by the fact that one of Paul's companions in the later years of his ministry was Luke the beloved physician (Colossians 4:14). But to my mind the decisive arguments are to be found in the letter to the Galatians.

Here Paul speaks of God's being "pleased to reveal his Son to me" (Galatians 1:15) and of a subsequent revelation (Galatians 2:2). In the middle of the letter Paul reminds his readers that "it was because of a bodily ailment that I preached the gospel to you at first; and though my condition was a trial to you, you did not scorn or despise me, but received me as an angel of God, as Christ Jesus. What has become of the satisfaction you felt? For I bear you witness that, if possible, you would have plucked out your eyes and given them to me" (Galatians 4:13-16).

Unlike some believers who feel that an admission of sickness is an admission of loss of faith and loss of face, Paul admits frankly his "bodily ailment." Moreover, his next remarks suggest that the affliction had something to do with his eyes. If they could have given him an eye transplant, they would have gladly done so!

Toward the end of the letter Paul makes a remark that at first sight seems curious: "See with what large letters I am writing to you with my own hand" (Galatians 6:11). The remark fits the suggestion that Paul could not see clearly enough to write ordinary, smaller writing. Defective eyesight may well help to explain why so many of Paul's letters were taken down by colleagues who acted as secretaries, and why Paul wrote personally only a word of greeting at the end. See, for example, Romans 16:22; 1 Corinthians 16:21; Colossians 4:18.

At the end of the letter to the Galatians Paul writes, "Henceforth let no man trouble me; for I bear on my body the marks [stigmata] of Jesus. The grace of our Lord Jesus Christ be with your spirit, brethren. Amen" (Galatians 6:17-18). Some have taken this to mean that Paul bore the stigmata of Christ in the sense of the wounds that Christ bore. But the first reported instance of this phenomenon is that of Francis of Assisi in the Middle Ages. There is no further indication in Paul's writings that this is what he had experienced. But, as we have seen, Paul's encounter with the risen Christ on the Damascus road left him blinded. He recovered his sight for the time being. But already when he first visited the Galatians and later when he wrote to them, Paul's sight seems to have been impaired.

Perhaps "the marks of Jesus" were the marks that were left on him by his encounter with Christ. They were part of the cost of Paul's discipleship. The marks were not removed. Whatever they were, they belonged to being "crucified with Christ" (Galatians 2:20). Yet pain and suffering were not the last word. What mattered was Christ living out his life in Paul the apostle. Paul's last word to the Galatians was not about suffering but about grace.

When he wrote to the Corinthians about his thorn in the flesh, Paul saw a reason for his suffering. It was to keep him from being too elated by the abundance of revelations (2 Corinthians 12:7). He could also describe it as "a messenger of Satan." Perhaps a voice told him that his suffering was not really deserved. Perhaps it said that he could not really be a true apostle and still suffer. Perhaps it suggested that if only the impediment were removed, he could serve Christ much better. Suffering is an evil. But suffering can be compounded by diabolical suggestions about its meaning.

We cannot be absolutely sure what Paul meant by his thorn in the flesh. What we can be sure of is that Paul prayed about it. He tells us: "Three times I besought the Lord about this, that it should leave me; but he said to me, 'My grace is sufficient for you, for my power is made perfect in weakness' " (2 Corinthians 12:8-9).

Paul's prayer was answered, but it was not answered in the way he had hoped. The weakness remained, but in it Paul experienced something greater. He experienced the grace of God. Paul's response to the fact that God did not remove the affliction was not one of depression or bitterness. It was exactly the opposite. He went on to say, "I will all the more gladly boast of my weaknesses, that the power of Christ may rest upon me. For the sake of Christ, then, I am content with weaknesses, insults, hardships, persecutions, and calamities; for when I am weak, then I am strong" (2 Corinthians 12:9-10).

Health and well-being are things we all want deep down inside ourselves. Nobody in his or her right mind wants the weaknesses, insults, hardships, persecutions, and calamities that Paul talks about here. We want success and happiness, not pain and anxiety. But life is full of paradoxes. We take so many things for granted until we lose them. We spend so much of our time chasing after things that do not satisfy us deep down. The miracle of grace is the miracle of the unexpected. God gives us many things—even sometimes the things that we want. But God can turn even the things that we dread into blessings. God's greatest gift is his love. When all is said and done, God's promise " 'My grace is sufficient' " is the best promise of all.

A Note on Books

The purpose of this note is to provide guidance to readers who wish to explore the question of miracles more deeply.

PHILOSOPHICAL AND THEOLOGICAL DISCUSSIONS OF MIRACLES

My larger study *Miracles and the Critical Mind* (Grand Rapids: Wm. B. Eerdmans, 1984) reviews the history of the controversy concerning Jesus' miracles from the early centuries to the present day from both the philosophical and the theological standpoints. Details of books and articles in English and other languages are given in the endnotes (pp. 327-74).

An important philosophical study of miracles is Richard Swinburne's *The Concept of Miracle* (London: Macmillan, St. Martin's Press, 1970). The most comprehensive review of the Gospel miracles is H. van der Loos, *The Miracles of Jesus, Supplements to Novum Testamentum IX* (Leiden: E. J. Brill, 1968). An older but still valuable study is Alan Richardson's *The Miracle-Stories of the Gospels* (London: S.C.M. Press, 1941). More recent critical viewpoints are represented by Gerd Theissen, *The Miracle Stories of the Early Christian Tradition* (Edinburgh: T. & T. Clark and Philadelphia: Fortress Press, 1983), and Howard Clark Kee, *Miracle in the Early Christian World* (New Haven and London: Yale University Press, 1983). *Miracles: Cambridge Studies in their Philosophy and History,* edited by C. F. D. Moule (London: A. R. Mowbray and New York: Morehouse-Barlow, 1965), contains discussions from scientific, historical, and theological stand-points. C. S. Lewis's *Miracles: A Preliminary Discussion* (London: Bles, 1947) is published in paperback by Macmillan.

Two important Roman Catholic treatments of mira-cles, which include discussions of miracles in the history of the church, are Louis Monden's *Signs and Wonders: A Study of the Miraculous Element in Religion* (New York: Desclée, 1966) and Leopold Sabourin's *The Divine Miracles Discussed and Defended* (Rome: Catholic Book Agency, 1977).

On the quest of the historical Jesus see Albert Schweitzer, *The Quest of the Historical Jesus,* reprint with an introduction by James M. Robinson that updates and as-sesses Schweitzer's work (New York: Macmillan, 1969); Colin Brown, *Jesus in European Protestant Thought, 1778-1860* (Durham, North Carolina: The Labyrinth Press, 1985); Dan-iel L. Pals, *The Victorian "Lives" of Jesus* (San Antonio, Texas: Trinity University Press, 1982); and Werner G. Kümmel, *The New Testament: The History of the Investigation of its Prob-lems* (Nashville: Abingdon Press, 1964).

On the question of "divine men" in the ancient world see D. L. Tiede, *The Charismatic Figure as Miracle Worker* (Missoula: Scholars Press, 1972), and C. H. Holladay, *THEIOS ANĒR in Hellenistic Judaism* (Missoula: Scholars Press, 1977). A major article that contains important material on the ques-tion of miracles and magic is David E. Aune's "Magic in Early Christianity." It is contained in *Aufstieg und Niedergang der römischen Welt,* II, 23, 2 (Berlin: Walter de Gruyter, 1980, pp. 1507-57). An important forthcoming study is the volume of essays by members of the Tyndale House Gospels Research Project edited by David Wenham and entitled *The Miracles of Jesus.* It will appear as Volume VI in the series *Gospel Perspectives* (published in Sheffield, England, by the *Journal for the Study of the Old Testament*).

Among the books dealing with science and religion are Bernard Ramm, *The Christian View of Science and Scripture* (Grand Rapids: Eerdmans, 1955); E. L. Mascall, *Christian*

Theology and Natural Science (London: Longmans, 1956); Ian G. Barbour, *Issues in Science and Religion* (Englewood Cliffs, NJ: Prentice-Hall, 1966); A. R. Peacocke, *Science and the Christian Experiment* (London: Oxford University Press, 1971); A. R. Peacocke, *Creation and the World of Science* (Oxford: Clarendon Press, 1978); Stanley L. Jaki, *The Road of Science and the Ways to God* (Chicago: University of Chicago Press, 1978); and John Polkinghorne, *The Way the World Is* (Grand Rapids: Eerdmans, 1983).

BOOKS ON MIRACLES AND HEALING

Among the older evangelical books that advocate a ministry of healing today are A. J. Gordon's *The Ministry of Healing: Miracles of Cure in All Ages* (1882) and A. B. Simpson's *The Gospel of Healing* (1915). Both books have been reprinted in paperback by Christian Publications of Harrisburg. Two older books from an Anglican perspective are Percy Dearmer's *Body and Soul* (New York: E. P. Dutton, 1909) and Evelyn Frost's *Christian Healing* (London: Mowbray, 1940). More recent are Jim Glennon's *Your Healing Is Within You* (London: Hodder and Stoughton, 1978) and *How Can I Find Healing?* (London: Hodder and Stoughton, 1984), and J. Sidlow Baxter's *Divine Healing of the Body* (Grand Rapids: Zondervan, 1979). Morton Kelsey shares his understanding of the history of religious healing in *Healing and Christianity in Ancient Thought and Modern Times* (New York: Harper and Row, 1973). The former Roman Catholic priest Francis McNutt is the author of the best-selling *Healing* (Notre Dame: Ave Maria Press, 1974) and its sequel *The Power to Heal* (Notre Dame: Ave Maria Press, 1977).

Studies that relate healing to the atonement and salvation include T. J. McCrossan's *Bodily Healing and the Atonement,* reedited by Roy Hicks and Kenneth E. Hagin (Tulsa: Faith Library, 1982), and John P. Baker's *Salvation and*

Wholeness: The Biblical Perspectives of Healing (London: Fountain Trust, 1973).

A major study from the standpoint of traditional Roman Catholic theology is Louis Monden's *Signs and Wonders,* which we have already noted. Monden argues that the Catholic Church has a virtual monopoly on miracles, and questions the claims outside his church. Another important Roman Catholic study is Leopold Sabourin's *The Divine Miracles Discussed and Defended,* also noted above.

General discussions of sickness, health, and healing from a theological perspective include Klaus Seybold and Ulrich B. Mueller, *Sickness and Healing* (Nashville: Abingdon, 1981); Martin E. Marty and Kenneth L. Vaux, editors, *Health Medicine and the Faith Traditions: An Inquiry into Religion and Medicine* (Philadelphia: Fortress Press, 1982); and John Wilkinson, *Health and Healing: Studies in New Testament Principles and Practice* (Edinburgh: The Handsel Press, 1980). An important collection of historical studies on special questions is the volume edited by W. J. Sheils, *The Church and Healing* (published for the Ecclesiastical History Society by Basil Blackwell, Oxford, 1982).

An older study of the demonic and exorcism is William Menzies Alexander's *Demonic Possession in the New Testament: Its Historical, Medical and Theological Aspects* (reprint Grand Rapids: Baker Book House, 1980). More recent studies include John Richards, *But Deliver Us from Evil: An Introduction to the Demonic Dimension in Pastoral Care* (London: Darton, Longman and Todd, 1974); John Warwick Montgomery, *Principalities and Powers: The World of the Occult* (Minneapolis: Dimension Books, 1975); Dom Robert Petitpierre, editor, *Exorcism: The Report of a Commission Convened by the Bishop of Exeter* (London: S.P.C.K., 1972); and the series of articles published in *The Churchman,* Volume 94, Number 3 (1980). Other interpretations of the demonic are given by S. V. McCasland, *By the Finger of God: Demon Possession in Early Christianity in the Light of Mod-*

ern Views of Mental Illness (New York: Macmillan, 1951), and Walter Wink, *Naming the Powers: The Language of Power in the New Testament* (Philadelphia: Fortress Press, 1984). Wink plans two further volumes to be entitled *Unmasking the Powers* and *Engaging the Powers.*

Among the studies that have subjected claims about healing to rigorous critical scrutiny and have returned negative verdicts are B. B. Warfield's *Miracles: Yesterday and Today, True and False* (1918; reprint Grand Rapids: Eerdmans, 1954) and D. J. West's *Eleven Lourdes Miracles* (London: Duckworth, 1957). A judicious caution on the whole subject is exercised by Henry W. Frost in *Miraculous Healing: A Personal Testimony and Biblical Study* (reprint London: Marshall, Morgan and Scott, with an appreciation by David Martyn Lloyd-Jones, 1951; Grand Rapids: Zondervan, 1979, foreword by Joni Eareckson). Lloyd-Jones set forth his own view in *The Doctor Himself and the Human Condition* (London: Christian Medical Fellowship, 1982). Among the shorter but nevertheless valuable studies are Vincent Edmunds and C. Gordon Scorer, *Some Thoughts on Faith Healing* (London: Inter-Varsity Press, 1956, and revised editions), and Gordon D. Fee, *The Disease of the Health and Wealth Gospels* (Costa Mesa: The Word for Today, 1979). A Roman Catholic study which draws on experience in the Third World is Aylward Shorter's *Jesus and the Witch Doctor: An Approach to Healing and Wholeness* (London: Geoffrey Chapman; New York: Orbis Books, 1985). The work of Kathryn Kuhlman and the activity of Filipino psychic surgeons has been scrutinized by William A. Nolen, M.D., in *Healing: A Doctor in Search of a Miracle* (New York: Random House, 1974).

Index of Names

229

Index of Subjects

Made in the USA
Middletown, DE
20 January 2023

22701529R00137